A GIFT OF DOUBT

A GIFT OF DOUBT

Struggles with Christian Faith and Uncertainty

ROBERT H. POPE

PRENTICE-HALL, INC., Englewood Cliffs, N.J.

Design by Janet Anderson

A GIFT OF DOUBT
Struggles with Christian Faith and Uncertainty
by Robert H. Pope • Copyright © 1971 by Robert H. Pope
All rights reserved. No part of this book may be reproduced
in any form or by any means, except for the inclusion of
brief quotations in a review, without permission in writing
from the publisher. • ISBN-0-13-354878-3 • Library
of Congress Catalog Card Number: 70-158192 • Printed
in the United States of America *T* • Prentice-Hall Inter-
national, Inc., London • Prentice-Hall of Australia, Pty.
Ltd., Sydney • Prentice-Hall of Canada, Ltd., Toronto
• Prentice-Hall of India Private Ltd., New Delhi •
Prentice-Hall of Japan, Inc., Tokyo

Dedicated to
a patient and loving congregation
that has helped me to grow in the Lord

"... Too much sanity may be madness. And maddest of all, to see life as it is and not as it should be."

MAN OF LA MANCHA

PREFACE

I AM A FIRST-GENERATION
Christian. Although I was sent to Sunday School as
a child, my family was not the least bit religious. I can recall
two things about my childhood Christianity: I couldn't bring
myself to believe all those miraculous stories they told me,
and I couldn't wait to grow up so that I wouldn't have to go
to church anymore. After I was out of high school I didn't
return to church until after a successful engineering career;
I entered seminary when I was thirty-five years old.

Now I say all this to avoid misunderstanding and condemnation of the church because of what I write and also to make
it clear that I am still growing and learning as a Christian,
which is really what this book is all about. It is a glimpse at
one man's struggle to understand the suburban ministry and
to understand his parish. It is the story of a struggle—not a
success story as most Christian books tell it—but a wrestling
match with all the doubts about the church, God, and oneself.
It is an account of one man's effort to make sense of the particular task and role of the suburban church in today's life.

I say struggle because I believe that is what the Christian
life is all about. To say it is anything less would be to confess a
naiveté about life or an indifference to the condition of men
and women in today's world, which would be worse than ad-

11

mitting the struggle in the first place. Besides, I am sure that this accounting of the Christian struggle is not far removed from Biblical experiences. I am a believer that Paul was not converted between chapters seven and eight of Romans (I do not speak from scholarship here, but from experience), but certainly he was describing an inner struggle against human passions which we all confront even as Christians. After all, who would agonize quite so much over his moral failures but one who will not be left alone by his conscience of faith? And who but a Christian, like Paul, would find he is somehow redeemed by some miraculous "resurrection" and not condemned? Which one of us has not at some time said to himself, if not to others, "Wretched man that I am! Who will deliver me from this body of death? Thanks be to God through Jesus Christ our Lord" (Romans 7:24,25).

I think it is time that we stop deluding ourselves into thinking that Christianity is supposed to be a solution to our problems, as if it were some kind of medicine that somehow makes us into supermen who are above the inner agony, caught up into some kind of full-time ecstasy. Christianity is not an answer—it is a way of life. A life not filled with answers but perhaps best described as a life spent preparing for the questions! Just before he went to the cross Jesus was able to say to his disciples, "Be of good cheer, for I have overcome the world," because he had spent his life preparing for that moment of agony on the cross. He *overcame* the question, "Why hast thou forsaken me?"—he did not *answer* it.

So I write this book in order to encourage frankness about the Christian life and the Christian Church. It is only when we have been frank about our faith, our doubts, our failures, our ignorance, our indifference that we shall become believable. Taking a clue from Jesus, it is only when one becomes vulnerable that the redemptive process becomes a power in life. Today we need to learn how to be closer to what we really are, in order that we have a chance to become greater than we are by the grace of God.

It is in this spirit that I write this book, which actually is based on a journal I kept at irregular times during my first years of life as a parish minister. From these sometimes agonizing weekly or monthly accounts I have taken a few situations, commented on them, and assigned to them what I thought to be an appropriate verse of scripture.

I wish to thank Mildred Halsey, our church secretary, for her willingness to do the typing, Isaac Rottenberg who encouraged me during the preparation of the manuscript, and the many others who contributed to my Christian growth in ways that will never be measured.

MY HOPE, of course, is that every reader will identify in some way with what is said on the following pages. The danger is, however, that some, particularly from my parish, will think of themselves or someone else as part of some particular incident. In order to avoid this, each situation, other than my own personal accounts, has been carefully altered to protect those actually involved.

FIRST YEAR

MARCH

MEN LIKE C continue to astound
me and scare me a little! He astounds me
because I believe that he is under the impression that all
these committees we have in the church are as important
and worthwhile as the meetings he has in his business.
He is so naive about what is going on. He takes these
meetings so seriously—in an innocent way.

This is why he scares me a little. Because he's bound to be
disillusioned and he's most likely to be disillusioned by my
indifference to the "business" of the church.

When he is, I hope he's not also disillusioned about Christ!

YOUR PROPHETS HAVE *seen for you false and deceptive*
visions; they have not exposed your iniquity to restore your
fortunes, but have seen for you oracles false and misleading.
All who pass along the way clap their hands at you; they
hiss and wag their heads at the daughter of Jerusalem; "Is
this the city which was called the perfection of beauty, the
joy of all the earth?" LAMENTATIONS 2:14,15 R.S.V.

THE TROUBLE IS that we try to convince ourselves that what
we are doing is meaningful and important and for our own
good so long as it is something we are doing for the "establishment." But sooner or later people discover that there is

17

no difference between working on a church board or on any other organizational board. In fact there is often a greater sense of sacrifice and service working on the local school board or town council or Little League committee *simply because there is no illusion of salvation.*

One wonders how many people have rolled up their sleeves ready to go to work for the "kingdom" by cutting the lawn, or painting the Sunday School, or making drapes for the social hall, only to find out that there is really nothing to this kind of "Christianity" after all? As one "pagan" witness said: "The only kind of participation that makes sense is for me to work here [in the hospital]. Churches are too social. They talk too much." She had discovered that many of our prophets were false—and the hiss and the wag of her head was discernible as she spoke.

We need to demythologize the Property Committee and the Ladies' Guild and the other auxiliaries. Then we will be putting our little organizations on the line and begin to discover what it means to lose our ecclesiastical life—
in order that lives might be really saved.

APRIL

I HAD A BRIEF and disturbing
conversation today. Mr. Z called to ask me
to say the invocation during the opening ceremonies of the Little League season. I made an excuse and suggested he find

18

someone who knew more about the game than I did—someone like himself, for instance! I was sure, I told him, this would make the prayers much more effective since he knew the players and the game well so. He said, on the contrary, "They need a priest or a minister—otherwise it might be interpreted that I [a layman] am imposing my religion on the public." I asked why he thought it would be any less true for a minister or a priest. He said, "Oh, but it's expected of you. You're part of a ceremony that everyone takes for granted!"

AGAIN, WHEN YOU *pray, do not be like the hypocrites; they love to say their prayers standing up in synagogue and at the street-corners, for everyone to see them. I tell you this: they have their reward already. But when you pray, go into a room by yourself, shut the door, and pray to your Father who is there in the secret place; and your Father who sees what is secret will reward you."*

MATTHEW 6:5,6 N.E.B.

I MUST CONFESS I have the greatest difficulty praying at civic occasions. One of the most meaningless tasks in the ministry is praying over buildings, cornerstones, luncheons, parades, athletic fields, etc. For one thing, I am never sure what I am supposed to be praying for or exactly to whom I am praying—I get the distinct impression that some of the elaborate and rhetorical monologues you sometimes hear are spoken to the public, not to the gods.

I say gods, because most civic leaders cover all the bets—all the gods, so to speak. When we all troop out—the priest, the rabbi, and the minister—with our own special version of the Diety, I feel as if we either don't trust one another in public or civic leaders are playing all the odds in the hope that at least one of us will get through to heaven.

Now, I know, of course, that civic leaders are simply being fair. It might be an offense to one of us if we were not included on a public occasion—which, of course, right away implies that it is not so much a matter of belief as it is protocol or tradition or propriety.

Yes, I'm afraid we are stuck with civic prayers. It is a part of our American landscape before any civic ceremony begins. It is simply expected that we will have a cleric place his blessings on the occasion. And we do the same thing in our churches.

Too often church people are dedication hounds. We dedicate everything from the communion rail to the dishwasher in the kitchen. Why? As near as I can discover, it is either to be sure that those who have donated an article to the church are properly recognized in public so that they will be willing to contribute again, or it is to help those who seldom contribute to summon up some feelings of shame or guilt because they give so little to the church.

So by treating it lightly, the significance of prayer is lost and we deserve what we get. What ever happened to Jesus' admonition about prayer—that it is a serious, even risky business which you should not treat lightly on a public platform? Rather you should go into your closet, shut the door, and know in the silence of your own thoughts and heart that the Lord, He is God.

We are confused about the very tools of our trade. We need to rethink our role in civic affairs, especially when it comes to prayers for all occasions.

*   *   *

YESTERDAY I PREACHED on faith and uncertainty and I discovered that I have no right to preach to people that way. I guess I have enough uncertainty (God knows!) to place me in the ranks of those in the pew, but not enough experience in the tragedies of life. In the sermon I suggested that the doubts that come out of tragedy are really prayers of faith like the epileptic boy's father who said, "I believe, help my unbelief." But that is intellectually easy for me to say since I have not been in all the dark places that many people in the pew have been. This is the most difficult part of preaching: to remain honest with oneself and those in the pew. Possibly, for that reason, preaching is a quite dishonest business!

DIVINE FOLLY IS *wiser than the wisdom of man, and divine weakness stronger than man's strength. My brothers, think what sort of people you are, whom God has called. Few of you are men of wisdom, by any human standard; few are powerful or highly born. Yet, to shame the wise, God has chosen what the world counts folly, and to shame what is strong, God has chosen what the world counts weakness. He has chosen things low and contemptible, mere nothings, to overthrow the existing order. And so there is no place for human pride in the presence of God. You are in Christ Jesus by God's act, for God has made him our wisdom; he is our righteousness; in him we are consecrated and set free. And so (in the words of Scripture), "If a man is proud, let him be proud of the Lord."* I CORINTHIANS 1:25-31 N.E.B.

HOW DO YOU STAY honest in the pulpit?

If I preach from my strength then my preaching necessarily becomes very limited, and if I preach from my weakness then people will not be fooled by my hypocrisy. How then do I preach about joy when I don't feel very joyful or how do I preach about love when I don't feel very loving? Even more significant, how do I preach to the layman who is *in* the world, demanding that he make certain sacrifices when I am not in his world? I cannot tell a man to go to work tomorrow and tell his boss that he will no longer have any part in seducing customers with women and booze at the local motel when I am nice and safe and secure at home with the women and children. No! If I preach about sacrifice then I must take the same risks that the layman is required to take. If I preach about joy, then I had better be joyful, and if I preach about peace, I had better be peaceful.

But there is a dangerous subtlety here. If I preach only from my strength, then I preach not out of love but from example—my example—and I don't have the humility for that!

No, the answer lies in being sure about God's grace above everything else. I must be an example of God's redemptive use of the sinner, not of personal character. People must know the whole preacher. They must know about my lack of courage, my infrequent joy, my feelings of guilt so that they will see the grace of God all the more. But as I say, it's a subtle thing. Preaching should not be maudlin any more than it should be proud. Perhaps the task *is* impossible, and for that reason grace from the pew is what a preacher counts on as much as the grace of God.

MR. AND MRS. T stared indignantly over the crowd as it pushed toward the door. Mr. T in particular hated crowds. He could remember as a child being caught in the press of adults rushing through a revolving door at a department store sale. Once he was in the door he couldn't escape—most of the women didn't even see him, tucked away in the crevice at the center—it wasn't until a very respectable, obviously well-bred woman noticed him from another quadrant of the door that he finally made his escape with her help. Ever since then Mr. T has had a contempt for crowds —especially the pushing and shoving kind which this one seemed to be.

The sermon had gone on too long and with three anthems this morning it was already fifteen minutes overtime; people were waiting for the next service outside. In fact they had gathered around the door to the point where it was difficult for those inside to make their way out. A fleeting thought passed Mr. T's mind that maybe the board ought to consider a revolving door so that the crowd could be handled with greater dispatch and people could enter and leave at the same time. But it was only one of those flashing moments of inspiration, because for just about every other Sunday of the year the crowds were not there. After all, this was Easter and Mr. T supposed one could put up with almost anything as long as it was only once a year. No, the expense was just too great to make it practical for one Sunday a year. Besides, wasn't it the obligation of the church to use its money wisely? After all, hadn't he demonstrated that when he had insisted that the new church be built on the outskirts of town where land was cheaper?

For the first time he noticed K ahead of him. Mr. T wondered when *he* was in church the last time. K always impressed him as someone who was very difficult to get along with—he always had such odd ideas about things. What had brought him to church this morning? He remembered hearing something about him being seriously ill a few months ago. Ah, well, Easter—everybody went to church on Easter. Maybe he had promised his wife. Some men are willing to suffer almost anything—as long as it's only once a year—to keep their wives happy. He felt sorry for Mrs. K. She came quite frequently in spite of her husband. Mr. T was glad he was able to go together with Mrs. T. He must make a point to speak to K before he got away. K was apparently quite successful in his business. As he recalled they had just bought a new house on the west side of town—he must have paid a fortune for it and he had his own business. Something to do with construction. Say, maybe K could help out with the new church! They could use a man like that! Too bad he only shows up on Easter. He could do a lot for the church. Mr. T wondered what kind of sickness K had had. Oh, well, he looked pretty good now.

"Hey, by golly, it's good to see you this morning!"

NEXT MORNING THE *crowd was standing on the opposite shore. They had seen only one boat there, and Jesus, they knew, had not embarked with his disciples, who had gone away without him. Boats from Tiberias, however, came ashore near the place where the people had eaten the bread*

24

over which the Lord gave thanks. When the people saw that neither Jesus nor his disciples were any longer there, they themselves went aboard these boats and made for Capernaum in search of Jesus. They found him on the other side. "Rabbi," they said, "when did you come here?" Jesus replied, "In very truth I know that you have come looking for me because your hunger was satisfied with the loaves you ate, not because you saw signs. . . ."   JOHN 6:22-26 N.E.B.

MR. T, OF course, is fictional. Yet much of Mr. T's thinking is far from fictional. Religious people have always attempted to manipulate others for their own purpose, even the crowds that followed Jesus tried it. Yet every time it is done, it is bound to reduce a person's humanity a bit. K, who is wanted for his wealth and influence, is less a man than he would be if he were wanted out of respect for him as a person. Anyone who knows he is accepted because of what he *has* rather than for what he *is* is bound to lose some respect for himself and others.

This, of course, becomes the prostitution of the church. Redemption of its people, the true goal of the church, is forsaken for the higher priority of buildings, budgets, and boosters. The prohibition that Alcoholics Anonymous groups have against owning things has the advantage that it prevents any confusion about the organization's purpose: the redemption of the alcoholic. Perhaps this is why AA is often a better example of Christianity at work than the church.

The church has a role that is reversed from that of most institutions in the world. The late President Kennedy's often quoted statement illustrates that reversal best; he said at his inauguration: "Ask not what your country can do for you; ask what you can do for your country." For the church, we might rather say, "Ask not what you can do for your church; ask what your church can do for you." We think rather consistently in terms of working to keep the church going rather than seeing the church as existing to keep people going out from it to be the salt that seasons life in the world.

That this has happened is understandable, especially in suburbia where the facade tends to be so thick. After all who wants to admit dependence on an organization? It does much more for the ego to be able to assure yourself that the organization just couldn't have built its new building without your energy and know-how. There are very few people around who are ready to admit they need something more, so we fall into the trap of working for the church. The church becomes the manipulator. The church becomes the end in itself.

And so more often than not the church becomes an empty shell with no power or spirit, a revolving door ushering people with nameless faces in and out. Bring your money, apply your talents, O lawyer, carpenter, electrician, businessman, but don't tell me your name. Don't tell me how you got out of bed this morning dreading the thought of facing the day. Don't tell me how you bleed inside because of your insincerity and infidelity. Don't show me your pain, just give me your talents and keep smiling and keep coming. Keep the pews and treasury filled and the grass cut and don't tell me about your heart because my own is about to break too.

What have we become? We have a name, *Christian*, but are we not really nameless? Have we not removed from the word "Christian" the power of Christ? We have made Christian nameless and we will remain nameless until we find the courage to name ourselves.

What shall we become? Ah, there is the question! We have to find words that help us to name ourselves. We need the courage to reveal better what we are and to recognize that we are each a microcosm of every man's doubts and pains. Maybe this is what Paul meant by his enigmatic statement that he was all things to all men. Perhaps he meant that through his life he had a part in the corruptions of all men and maybe we have to admit that too before we shall deserve to name ourselves Christians.

JUNE

JUST RETURNED FROM a clergy luncheon, and I came away with a curious feeling that we were not all being honest with one another. The jokes were plentiful and there were the usual polite comments about how hard it was to get church school teachers and how apathetic people were about social concerns. But I couldn't help feeling an uneasiness. It was superficial. When there are too many jokes and too much laughter, I'm always uneasy. Maybe it's me. Maybe I take things too seriously and don't laugh enough, but my intuition tells me in these kinds of circumstances, too many jokes are often a way of avoiding something else. And maybe what we are avoiding is the underlying fact that we are in competition with one another and therefore we don't really trust each other. If this is the case, then the testimony is clear, we have a great deal to learn about Christ!

The major topic of conversation was one which had apparently been discussed before: "How do we get religion into public schools?" Now here is an interesting issue if the above is true; because any program which includes people from all denominations must be carefully contrived so that we are all protected from each other. This is why the conversation quickly got around to a "released time" program which would allow students to be dismissed from school for an hour a week to go to their churches or synagogues for special instruction. This would protect our traditions and there would be a token integration of religion into secular education. But I can't help feeling there has to be a better way and we are just not seeing it because we are too self-protecting. If this is the case we no doubt have a long way to go in our relationships and our "religion," which, after all, is supposed to make us the examples of social conscience. If, for example, we urge the white man to trust that the black man will not ghettoize suburbia if he moves in next door, but we fail to trust a brother Christian who is white and already our neighbor, our words will quickly lose their integrity. And we will eventually lose our traditions and our religious lives because no one will listen to our words nor pay much attention to our actions.

THEN PHARISEES AND *scribes cames to Jesus from Jerusalem and said, "Why do your disciples transgress the tradition*

*of the elders? For they do not wash their hands when they
eat." He answered them, "And why do you transgress the
commandment of God for the sake of your tradition?"*

WHAT OUR PREOCCUPATION with released time all boils down
to is a lack of faith in our own traditions. We are afraid
to expose them, even to one another! We don't trust one
another enough to deal with them openly. I'm sure one of
the major reasons why we cannot integrate secular and religious education is not because secular educators are "god-
less," but more because of our own unwillingness to lay our
traditions on the line, to put them to the test. In fact I often
find myself on the side of the secular educators. They have
a point: balking when we want to take up *their* time to teach
our own private points of view. Praise the Lord, the Supreme
Court protects our schools from that!

But there is much than can be done to relate secular and
religious education. The mistake we make is trying to get
our own style of shoe in the schoolroom door; rather, we
should let the schools into the church door. Once we start
thinking this way all kinds of possibilities open up for us.

Public education deals with the human spirit. At least it
should, and to varying degrees it does. The arts, literature,
social sciences try to describe it, organize it, and predict it.
Such powerful influences should not be ignored by the
church.

Take literature, for instance. Would it not be much more
sensible if the church began to have classes in English
Literature rather than the schools having classes in religion?
If the church were to conduct a class which met to discuss

the very same novels being read in public school a great deal could be accomplished. Two immediate advantages are evident: the student should improve his English grade with the extra tutoring while not having an added homework burden since he would already have read the book for public school; but most especially, the church would at last be trying to relate the Christian faith to something the student is dealing with in public life and the student would tend to see the meaning of the Christian faith more plainly with the illustrative help of contemporary novels. Much of the literature being read in public schools deal with the questions that we are supposed to be experts at: sin, salvation, human destiny, the problem of suffering, etc. Would it not be more practical and exciting and challenging to try to relate our faith to the human questions and problems they raise?

We could go even further. We could organize our church high-school curriculum around the public education curriculum. When the schools talk about Darwin, we should be talking about Darwin too (for example, the survival of the fittest vs. blessed are the meek). When Karl Marx comes along in public school, his social principles should be examined in church school. This, of course, further applies to the great questions of science and faith, determinism and free will, secular history and redemptive history. Here indeed is a wealthy resource of Christian education with the advantage that it's relevant (in the best sense of that overused word): the student who spends half his life in public school discovers, possibly for the first time, that the church is concerned with what he does and in fact relates to what he is doing.

But I understand why we are reluctant. We don't have all the answers and we are afraid of that kind of exposure. We are afraid we will be cornered and people will find out that religion doesn't know everything. This is the same reason we tell so many jokes in our ministerial get-togethers—we are afraid. Afraid that someone will prove us wrong, afraid that our traditions and doctrines will fail us. So we protect ourselves by being nice guys, slapping everyone on the back, telling each other how great we are, laughing all the time. But if we could just begin to laugh at ourselves a little and maybe begin to open ourselves to each other then I am sure we would quickly discover how very much more we could do for the sake of the Kingdom.

_____ OCTOBER _____

I AM BECOMING more and more
aware of how destructive religion can be.
Here is a very "religious" family sitting on a powder keg of emotion, anxiety, and tension, and there is little that anyone can do about it. Their "religion" blocks any hope of reaching them. They have a sort of tragic fear about revealing their need because it would mean confession that God had somehow failed them.
People with this kind of fundamental "non-faith" often

31

raise barriers to wholeness because they will not let themselves believe their "religion" has let them down. When they are confronted with situations that threaten to expose their inability to live a joyful or peaceful or loving life, they withdraw. They hide from reality because their religion dictates that one who has found salvation is necessarily happy, peaceful, and loving.

They have assumed that any action of theirs which denies the utopian dream that Christ in some magical way solves all our problems is blasphemy. They can hardly admit their faith has failed them—if they do, their religious house of cards collapses.

In this case the arrogance and dogmatism of one member of the family conflicts with the sensitivity and surface emotion of another. The tensions in the family must be tremendous. It is in situations like this that I get an overwhelming feeling of helplessness. No approach seems to break through the protective wall of religion—God help them and us!

AND SAMUEL SAID, *"Though you are little in your own eyes, are you not the head of the tribes of Israel? The Lord anointed you king over Israel. And the Lord sent you on a mission, and said, 'Go, utterly destroy the sinners, the Amalekites, and fight against them until they are consumed.' Why then did you not obey the voice of the Lord? Why did you swoop on the spoil, and do what was evil in the sight of the Lord?"* And Saul said to Samuel, *"I have obeyed the voice of the Lord, I have gone on the mission on which the Lord sent me, I have brought Agag the king of Amalek, and I have utterly destroyed the Amalekites. But the people took*

32

*of the spoil, sheep and oxen, the best of the things devoted
to destruction, to sacrifice to the Lord your God in Gilgal."
Then Samuel said, "Bring here to me Agag the king of the
Amalekites." And Agag came to him cheerfully. Agag said,
"Surely the bitterness of death is past." And Samuel said,
"As your sword has made women childless, so shall your
mother be childless among women." And Samuel hewed
Agag in pieces before the Lord in Gilgal.*

I SAMUEL 15:17-21,32,33 R.S.V.

SAMUEL HAD AN absolute view of religion that literally
destroyed Agag! I wonder how often that point of view has
destroyed people in much more subtle ways. How often has
"righteous indignation" turned a "sinner" to deeper sin? How
often has the stigma of righteousness kept an unrighteous
man out of church? How often has the idea that we must
live up to some external standard of purity caused the
Christian to become a false god unto himself?

Certainly, too often our religious attitudes cause people
to become tense and fearful and they withdraw from any
real encounters. By our actions or words, sometimes quite
unconsciously done or said, we convince one another of our
purity and righteousness and knowledge; and for fear of
appearing depraved, unworthy, and stupid in the light of
each other's superiority, we withdraw from honest confrontation. We do not allow our facades to be penetrated
and we live in hell, whether we know it or not. Somehow
we have to tell people about our love of Christ, but at the
same time tell them how *we* fail and how very much we
need His kind of love, compassion, and justice. Somehow we
even have to find the courage to shake our fist at God to

let Him know that we are tired of living in hell. Somehow we have to discover how to be open and free and spontaneous.

But how do you contrive openness? You don't! That's one of our biggest problems as a church. That's the problem with "organized religion." You cannot organize what we need the most. You can not bring people to the point where they discover relationships that are warm, believable, frank, and enduring by means of a system—at least any system that doesn't have a whole lot of leeway in it—especially if we are all just learning how to be open, warm, believable, and frank!

The trouble with most churches is that they are so well organized they are impersonal. Isn't it better to become less and less organized in order to build in more and more of a chance of spontaneous encounter?

Spontaneity, that's what's missing! That's what the early church had that we don't have enough of. If two people respond without thinking with sincere sympathy to a bereaved woman who has just lost her husband, is it not far more genuine and therefore more believable than ten people from, say, the altar guild paying a call because that's their job?

But how do we get to the point where we get this kind of spontaneity? I don't know the answer to that. Much has been said about koinonia groups—Christian study and "encounter" sessions—but I'm not sure they will be enough.

It is perhaps more a matter of tenacious perseverance. It is something we have to work at constantly—urging, pleading, demonstrating to people. We have to consistently try to summon up enough openness so that the Spirit of God can come in and do something with us which is beyond all our contrivance.

There's an urgency to all this. People are starving for the Spirit because of their own rigidity. Perhaps that is the reason for the frustration. God help us to learn how to be free enough to love one another—and don't be too long doing it, Lord!

NOVEMBER

I BURIED J today. It was a sad affair. J was a woman in the prime of life with a child who already needed plenty of loving. Her husband was genuinely grief-stricken, but at the same time curiously buoyant. A strange incident occurred right after the service. The close relatives were about to view the body for the last time and the tears were flowing. J's mother had just come back from her last look and J's husband started to break down. She immediately turned to him and said, "Now, we mustn't get upset. We must be brave."

And like a little soldier he straightened up in his chair and threw his nose in the air and said, as if struck with a jolt of electricity, "Yes, yes, we must do that. We will be all right now."

This explained one thing to me. Why J found it so difficult

to show any signs of weakness, even in her last days. She had an unfortunate pride which would not even let her cry out when faced with death. This is also why her husband kept saying everything was fine as she lay dying in the hospital.

This adds to the grief even more. The real tragedy is to live with the ridiculous notion that we are really independent of the rest of the world. It is tragic because it not only makes for some of the most lonely people in the world, but it also makes for a very destructive society.

Maybe this is America's most negative contribution to humanity. Our pride has always had isolationist, self-made overtones. This destroys people—it places them in the very real hell of living with the horror of themselves with no outlets. J died a very unhappy woman because she thought of herself as independent and self-made, which is an illusion. None of us are self-made. Poor J was formed and molded by her mother's fear of exposed emotion, which she assumed was a sign of weakness, and thus she concluded that the way to live was by one's own stamina and resolution. She built a very high wall against the world which was to a large degree created by her mother.

Her last confession to me must have taken a great deal of courage.

NO LONGER, THEN, *do we judge anyone by human standards. Even if at one time we judged Christ according to human standards, we no longer do so. When anyone is joined to Christ he is a new being: the old is gone, the new has come. All this is done by God, who through Christ changed us from enemies into his friends, and gave us the task of mak-*

ing others his friends also. Our message is that God was making friends of all men through Christ. God did not keep an account of their sins against them, and he has given us the message of how he makes them his friends.

II CORINTHIANS 5:16-19 A.B.S.

CONCEIVABLY, SARTRE was wrong. Hell can sometimes be other people, but it is more than likely living with oneself without other people. There are people who live without relating to any other human being and who get along quite well in this world, but I can't believe they are really the fortunate ones. The fortunate ones are those who learn to relate.

Not that it's easy to learn. Some people are impossible to relate to, but the point is in the trying and finding some people who communicate. It doesn't seem to me that Jesus related to everybody—otherwise, he wouldn't have ended up on the cross—but he communicated to a few so powerfully that they were changed men, inspired and liberated.

There is a certain redemptive quality in a good relationship and this is what makes it so important. Some people have a greater natural capacity for this than others. It's like being a born musician. You either feel the music or you don't. Some have a natural feel for other people, others have to work harder at it, and, of course, some never work at it at all.

But this is where the community of believers becomes so important, because it should be the one place in the world where people can find the greatest encouragement for self-expression. The Church is the place where there should be the greatest of all possibilities for "becoming." We should

37

be able to say to anyone, "Here in this place there is nothing that you can say which is too blasphemous; here there are no words which are unspeakable; here you can express your ignorance, your doubts, your fears, your hates, your needs, your hopes, and your dreams, and you will only find love in return."

That is what we should be able to say, but we cannot; and because we cannot, people continue to live in the agony of loneliness. Sin continues "to have a man by himself," as Bonhoeffer put it, because there is no community where he can discover the difference of acceptance.

And this is our sin. We have failed to make clear "the message of how he makes them his friends."

And they die already in hell.

SECOND YEAR

LENT AND EASTER
are over. Thank God we are heading
into the summer slows. I look forward to it.

For a time I thought this particular season, which under-
lines Christ's passion and resurrection, wasted, but as it
turned out I learned a great deal.

We had our usual mid-week Lenten worship with guest
preachers which allowed me the luxury of sitting in the pew
and listening for a change. We asked them all to speak on
the general theme, "The Social Challenges in the Light of
the Faith of Our Time." For six weeks one basic message
emerged: "The church has got to get out into the world!"
Which means that Christians must make effective—in all
the back alleys, ghettos, business offices, etc.—their reconciling, compassionate, loving, understanding spirit. By the
sixth week I found myself both bored and irritated. I have
now come to realize what a meaningless message it is to
tell people they have to get out into the world.

If someone were to analyze it, they would find that we
preachers are really talking to ourselves when we say this.
It is the clergy who are less likely to be "in the world" than
the person in the pew and therefore it is a somewhat hypocritical message for those in the pew to hear.

For instance, it occurred to me the other day that being one step removed from the market place, we are in a far more secure position than the average commuting suburbanite. Since most of us do not own real estate it is already assumed that we will speak far more courageously when it comes to exposing the myth of the deterioration of property values in integrated neighborhoods. No matter how eloquent and convincing our words, our *lack of vulnerability* says something different to the listener. We are, after all, not really so much "in the world" as our congregations.

But if part of the problem is *our* security, the rest of the problem is the insecurity of the average churchgoer. In order for the church to be out in the world, in any reconciling or healing role, the people in it must experience some degree of wholeness themselves. The sad truth is that there are very, very few who are prepared!

How can we be reconcilers if we have not reconciled ourselves with our wife or daughter or son? How can we be the healing force that helps the guilty and fearful and lonely when we know very little about forgiveness and courage and fellowship? How can we love people who have very little in common with us (culturally, socially, etc.) when we have not learned to love those with whom we have a great deal in common? How can we exemplify Christ if we do not know him ourselves? You simply cannot ask a man, who has so many personal problems that he doesn't know how to begin to resolve them, to take on the burdens of the world and expect that there will be any meaningful results. "And if a blind man leads a blind man, both will fall into a pit" (Matthew 15:14). It is like asking a man with a sprained ankle to run the hundred-yard dash—he'll never make it. It's meaningless and commits the sin of insensitivity to other people's needs to insist that he try.

Of course, it is not to say that we all need to be righteous and perfect and good before we go into the back alleys of the world. (If that were true *nothing* would happen!) No, there is something to say for the wounded being more understanding to the wounded than those who have not been hurt in the battle. (The wounded who have been healed, that is! An open wound makes us far too subjective to be very effective lovers.) So if we are to be anything like what we think we ought to be in the world, there must come some degree of healing to the church itself. Without reasonably whole and well people we can not even begin to talk about carrying protest signs against the injustices of the world. Without healing, there is no "social" ministry. Without healing, there is no Gospel!

IS THERE NO *balm in Gilead?*
Is there no physician there?
Why then has the health of the daughter
of my people not been restored? JEREMIAH 8:22 R.S.V.

COULD IT BE that there is no balm in Gilead because most of us avoid the issue of healing? This is understandable. It's a matter of survival sometimes. It is better to avoid the personal needs of people and retreat to the pedestal, or become chaplain of the volunteer firemen, or tell jokes at the Ladies' Guild than it is to suffer the agony of facing people's needs, more often than not with empty hands.

The fact is, we are simply not prepared to deal with all the broken and unhappy marriages, the neurotic young people, the mentally frustrated housewives, the ethically guilty men, the mentally sick and destitute, the lonely, the aged, the hateful, the envious, the just plain scared people we meet every day. Sometimes I feel like I have nothing to offer but tears. "Rejoice with those who rejoice, weep with those who weep," says Paul (Romans 12:15). But is that enough? Can we endure plain sympathy and nothing else? Sooner or later our impotency catches up and we are reduced to our own guilts for having failed to confront people with any real healing power.

If we, the church, have any healing balm to offer the broken human being, then we had better get on with it. If we haven't, then all our talk is in vain and Christ is reduced to nothing very special at all. "But if there is no resurrection of the dead, then Christ has not been raised . . . and your faith is in vain," says Paul (I Corinthians 15:13,14). It would seem that it is a question of whether or not those who are the walking dead and wounded can really be resurrected. If we don't have a power in addition to the world's power to heal, then we have nothing. If we simply rely on clinics, psychiatrists, hospitals, to save us, we have no savior at all.

P is a fearful man. He is afraid of germs, his wife getting raped, his children catching cold, his car getting nails in its tires—he is afraid of many things. Now P is a man who knows the Gospel—at least he says he knows it—but knowing it has *increased* his fears. Now he has something else to worry about along with everything else. Now he is afraid to ask any real questions about God or the Bible for fear that maybe even the Gospel has no answers. P confesses Jesus Christ as savior and is dogmatically sure of it, but P has found no healing grace. Instead the very power that

44

could heal has become simply another fear along with all the rest. The Gospel without healing (resurrection!) is a dead Gospel and offers us nothing but more of the same.

Healing! This is where the frustrations and agony and the moment of truth is for the Christian Church and here is where I cannot help but feel God is calling me to be. God help me!

MAY

WE HAD AN interesting inter-change between L and D last night during our study session which helped clarify the problem of healing. We were talking about Jesus' statement, "He who saves his life loses it, and he who loses his life for my sake will save it." L interpreted this to mean action. The purpose of faith is an active willingness to sacrifice one's own security in terms of time, money, energy for the sake of other people. But D pointed out that realistically this is impossible for many people to do. Some people simply can't give their lives away—they can't risk that kind of exposure because they are too insecure and threatened already.

Both of these views (which I believe are completely right) reflect the personalities of both people. L is an activist. He attempts to act out the drama of redemption. But L is sometimes so concerned with "doing" that he borders on a lack of understanding and sensitivity to other people. So D is right also. D is a person who is in touch and understands people well. She can see their needs and pains and hurts and she tries to minister to them. L sees the great causes and injustices. D sees the individual. We need L's who are the doers and D's who are the healers. Between them both maybe there is an answer for the parish: through people like D we can be helped to understand ourselves better and receive compassionate encouragement so that through people like L we can be led to do what we have always feared to do.

But another lesson to be learned from all this is that we cannot afford to be too dogmatic about the gospel. We cannot say dogmatically that Christianity is social action any more than we can say Christianity is personal salvation. The plain fact is that we must be willing to see and understand the person and apply what we know about Jesus Christ so that ears will hear and eyes will see within their capacity for hearing and seeing. We are not all the same except perhaps in our need for the healing and loving power of God, and *somehow* we must try to reveal this to each person as he comes to us.

WHEN JESUS WAS *at table in his house, many bad characters— tax-gatherers and others—were seated with him and his disciples; for there were many who followed him. Some doctors of the law who were Pharisees noticed him eating in this bad company, and said to his disciples, "He eats with tax- gatherers and sinners!" Jesus overheard and said to them, "It is not the healthy that need a doctor, but the sick; I did not come to invite virtuous people, but sinners."*

MARK 2:15-17 N.E.B.

DID JESUS MEAN that there are righteous people who need no physician? No! He meant that there are some people who *think* they are righteous and who do not know they need a physician. Since no one is truly Christlike, no one is without need of a physician. It is rather a matter of degree. It is a matter of what level you are able to function on. To what degree are you able or willing to move and work and live and think beyond yourself? That is the question. That is the question for the congregation as well as the individual. The health of a congregation is measured by the extent to which it can operate beyond itself. Elaborate church buildings keep us from going beyond a certain level of congregational maturity. By their very existence they force us back to a concern for ourselves because they too must be cared for. Which is to say, to a large degree, the level of maturity that a congregation is able to achieve is limited by the size of its mortgage! It is our task to increase our individual and corporate ability to think beyond such concerns. This is the business of healing. Healing helps us to move more and more beyond our own concerns and our own worlds.

But how do we move in this direction? How do we break out of our personal, confining, limited worlds? There is no clear-cut, precise answer. Certainly we all have our particular hang-ups that keep us from maturity, and it may be that we will never rid ourselves of some of them completely, but that is not to say we can't move a long way toward wholeness if given the right medicine. What is the way to healing?

I have become convinced that one of the keys to healing is *acceptance*. It is a curious thing, but often the more neurotic people are the ones that seem to hear the Gospel of

47

acceptance the quickest and clearest. The stable, secure, calm people are the most difficult to affect in any significant way. I offer a humble explanation of this: the people who hear the quickest are those who sense an element of personal acceptance and who have for most of their lives known very few people who have really accepted them. God speaks best to those who have experienced very little acceptance by this world. "Many tax collectors and sinners were sitting with Jesus and his disciples. . . ." Jesus knew how to accept the unaccepted people and restore their self-respect and humanity.

As a youngster I did not experience the liberating effect of acceptance. I felt very inadequate for many reasons. I felt unable to measure up to the standards set by family and peers. I was convinced of my own inadequacy and so also became convinced that no one really accepted me—and the more I felt this, the poorer I performed. I had a reputation for mediocrity and failure. But graduation from high school was the beginning of my liberation from all that. I went into military service and began to become aware of something very important. I discovered under this completely new set of circumstances that I was accepted by my peers as someone who was worth their company and comradeship, and so I began gradually to uncover the myth of my own inferiority and unacceptability. Knowing a group of people who accepted me as a person was the beginning of a renewed self-confidence and a more constructive life.

Now the church above all institutions is supposed to be a place where people such as sinners and tax-gatherers and whores are very welcome and accepted. (Note again Mark 2:15-17.) If only this were true! We as a people would become very attractive indeed. And we would have power. We would be bound to impress a great number of people because many are spiritually poverty-stricken because of their fear of rejection, judgment, criticism. After all it often begins very early in life—my own example is not unusual. Even in the classroom children are conditioned to fear the mocking criticism of teacher and peers when they don't perform according to the standards expected of them. So instead of being free to openness about what we know and feel, we clam up because we are fairly sure, judging from our experience, that the world would not accept us if it knew what we really thought and what we are really like. And we are right. The world will not accept us. The world will only accept the facade which we present to the general public. There is a real lack of genuineness in the world and this appears for some reason especially so in America.

So when an "unacceptable" person discovers that there is a group of people, or even one or two persons, who are willing to accept him as he is, he is bound to be impressed. He is bound to very quickly recognize that there is something different about these people that he has never (or rarely) experienced before in the world. He knows very quickly because all his life he has been unacceptable so he is supersensitive about it. You can bet on the fact that when it comes to acceptance he can read you like a book.

Of course there is a problem here: obviously you can't accept and be completely tolerant of someone who cruelly beats his children, or someone who is viciously bigoted and intolerant of other people. In other words, there must be a limit to tolerance or else we can not remain faithful to truth. In a sense, we can not compromise with evil without perpetuating evil ourselves. So how do we accept people without approving of what they are doing wrong? How do you love the sinner and hate the sin—as that old cliché goes?

Here we must again take a clue from Jesus. Take, for instance, his encounter with the Samaritan prostitute (John 4) at the well. This episode illustrates how to be accepting of the person without approving the evil he or she has done. And the key is this: Jesus was judgmental—he made note of the fact that she had not one husband, but many—*but* he was also accepting. He was accepting because he indirectly told her of her own worthiness by taking her into his confidence about himself. Up until then he had not revealed himself to anyone; then, to a woman who slept in every hut in the village, to this very "unacceptable" woman, to this very unlikely person who happens to be rejected and looked down on by all the "respectable" people, to her, he tells of his Messiahship.

We express acceptance when we are willing to reveal something of ourselves, when we take people into our confidence, when we make ourselves *vulnerable* to them and place our reputations or our weaknesses in their hands. Then we are saying in a very real way: I trust you. I respect you. I see in you something very worthwhile. And there is bound to be power in your willingness to accept people by giving them a part of yourself. After all, there never is any real loving without that.

We, of course, are not Jesus, so our revelations about ourselves must be quite different. We have to be ready to recognize that we are a part of everyone's sin, that we too have the scraps of every corruption in us, and be willing to hazard the revelation of our particular offense when it is

50

necessary to do so. We need to learn how to lead open lives. The key to acceptance, without approval, is to be as equally judgmental about ourselves as we are of other people and as willing to take the risk of exposure as much as we expect other people to take that same risk.

Well, how do we do all this as a congregation? Maybe this is not something we learn so much as it is something that we grow up too. Maybe it's a question of maturity again—that ability to live and move beyond oneself. It's our own fears that keep us from being accepting. *We must learn how to become vulnerable. That's the problem!* And maybe we learn to risk this kind of exposure best through a God who thought vulnerability to be so important that he willingly went all the way with it—even to the point of dying on the cross. Teach us how, Lord!

JUNE

IT'S UNBELIEVABLE HOW deeply we sin out of ignorance or neglect. Sometimes, I think, it's because we don't really want to know. We put the difficult parts of life out of our minds and hope they go away somehow. There is a polio case we all know about, she has been paralyzed from the neck down for eleven years. Ever since I've been here, whenever a page turner was men-

51

tioned, everyone said, "Well, she doesn't read much." And what astounds me is that I accepted that explanation. Of course she doesn't read much. How could she? It takes only a moment, and eleven years wasted. Tragic!

W made two phone calls. Two phone calls and he had a page turner—without even leaving his living room sofa—and ironically he obtained that service for nothing! The sin of failing to question our judgment, the sin of ignorance, the sin of neglect is upon all of us. God forgive us and maybe she will too!

SALT IS A *good thing; but if salt itself becomes tasteless, what will you use to season it?*   LUKE 14:34 N.E.B.

SOMETIMES WE BECOME tasteless, and do incredibly stupid things just because we accept what we hear without question. This is sin. It is sin not to question, accepting everything wide-eyed and innocent.

It's a sin, for instance, for a Christian to be innocent about what the world is like. Many like to project an image of piety and innocence, of a certain naiveté about some situations. Either this is a good act or it means that they have led incredibly sheltered lives. Either way it's sinful because it means they have not attempted to communicate enough, which means they haven't cared enough.

I remember talking to one minister about death and he was saying that only Christians were able to die courageously. I pointed out that I had witnessed a man on his deathbed reject God and die more courageously than I ever will.

"Well," he said, "I'll have to go back and check my books about that!"

The trouble is we talk to ourselves too much. We lull ourselves into an unconsciousness. We mesmerize ourselves into believing without question until we come to the point where we believe absurdities. And this is terribly destructive because it simply proves to the world that we are deluded.

It's all well and good to be fools for Christ (that is, to go against the world), but no one ever asked us to be fools. Jesus never once said anything that did not take into account the realities of life. There was no foolish naiveté about Jesus. He was a man who knew what the world was like. Jesus never came to the conclusions he did through wide-eyed innocence. He never could have challenged the establishment as he did if he didn't question everything.

Getting people to question the conclusions of men is important because it tends to uncover corruption, ignorance, and neglect. But getting people to question the principles of faith is necessary too, because without letting the waves of the world's doubts test our faith and convictions we fail Him by assuming an innocence which fools no one.

NOVEMBER

LAST NIGHT WE had our Bible Study group again. It was a wide-open discussion—we got off the subject very quickly. We were all wrestling with the question, it seems to me, of what the promise of the Christian Gospel is in this life. I don't believe anyone was speaking out of a vacuum. We all had been touched at some time or other, but no one could easily put it into words. Is it pure joy, peace, contentment? Are these the objectives of our faith? Surely Jeremiah was filled with anxieties and guilts and fears. . . .

It seems to me, particularly at this time, that the brokenness in life is far too evident to believe that Christianity is supposed to result in some kind of utopian bliss. There are just too many bleeding people. There are too many marriages that exist in anger; there are too many parents who, it would seem almost deliberately, have convinced their children that there is an irreconcilable barrier between them; there are too many children who cry because of the brutality they see between a mother and father; there are too many lonely people who, though they live and work in the community, are nonetheless bleeding inside because they are convinced that there is no place for them in anyone's dreams; there are the numerous fearful people who hide behind their shields of ego, or bluster, or busyness; there are too many people who have "solved" their problems with booze or a mistress or the golf course—there are just too many hurting people to think that there is much hope for this peace and tranquility that often emerges from sentimental Protestantism.

Whenever I run across a "born-againer" who has that certain smile on his face, gleam in his eye, hymn on his lips, Bible in his hand, skip in his step, I cannot help but be skeptical. Either he is deluded or he has never really looked at life and seen the pain in it. If he is genuine, he must be the world's most insensitive man. And I don't knock "bornagainers" because I was reborn, God knows! But to me, to be born again also means to be given a new place from which to look at life, a different point of view. It means becoming *more* aware of the pain—not less. It means facing life head-on with a new set of values. Life becomes a new ball game, one which at first is very unfamiliar, where the rules deliberately favor the other guy. Conversion is the chance to reorient oneself to a new, more loving, more sensitive perspective—but at the same time to feel the pain all the more. I am utterly convinced this kind of reorientation requires a power from God because it is too distressing for me alone to face.

I am very tired this morning. I am mentally and spiritually tired. It seems to me, at this moment at least, that I am not going to be able to say anything about the good when the evil is so overwhelming. I have a deep sense of inadequacy right now: I don't listen enough; I'm not smart enough; I'm not sensitive enough; I don't know enough about life and its persistent resurrections. Come, Lord Jesus!

AS SOON AS *they saw Jesus the whole crowd were overcome with awe, and they ran forward to welcome him. He asked them, "What is this argument about?" A man in the crowd spoke up: "Master, I brought my son to you. He is possessed by a spirit which makes him speechless. . . . I asked your disciples to cast it out, but they failed." Jesus answered: "What an unbelieving and perverse generation. . . . Bring him to me." . . . Jesus asked his father, "How long has he been like this?" "From childhood," he replied; "often it has tried to make an end of him by throwing him into the fire or into water. But if it is at all possible for you, take pity*

upon us and help us." "If it is possible!" said Jesus. "Every-
thing is possible to one who has faith." "I have faith," cried
the boy's father; "help me where faith falls short." Jesus saw
then that the crowd was closing in upon them, so he re-
buked the unclean spirit. "Deaf and dumb spirit," he said,
"I command you, come out of him and never go back!"
After crying aloud and racking him fiercely, it came out; and
the boy looked like a corpse; in fact, many said, "He is
dead." But Jesus took his hand and raised him to his feet,
and he stood up. MARK 9:15-27 N.E.B.

IN A KIND of prayer of gratefulness, Otto Dibelius once said,
"Lord my God, your word preserved me from skepticism and
contempt, those characteristics of an age alienated from
God." It would be easy to become a cynic, and Dibelius is
right, the only thing that keeps me from that fate is God
himself. It is he who helps me where my "faith falls short."

It's grace that saves me from total despondency, disappointment, and cynicism. Life is an experience of little resurrections and maybe that is as it should be.

I suppose I have within myself the unfortunate combina-
tion of practicality and idealism. I want to apply the ideal in
a practical way. This is, to say the least, a disillusioning
philosophy. Better to be as the late President Kennedy once
claimed for himself: "an idealist with no illusions." But in
many ways we need more idealists around today. There are
too many people compromising everything. America was
built on the great compromise. Compromise is the defeat
of hope . . . yet an unyielding ideal is the demagogue of
reason. Perhaps the answer lies somewhere in between.
Mark Gibbs once commented that what the church needs to

learn is "righteous compromise." Maybe a better word for that is grace.

The thoughts of the priest in Graham Greene's book, *The Power and the Glory*, say something about grace:

> *In any case, even if he could have gone south and avoided the village, it was only one more surrender: the years behind him were littered with similar surrenders. . . . Five years ago he had given way to despair—the unforgivable sin—and he was going back now to the scene of his despair with a curious lightening of heart. For he had gotten over his despair too. He was a bad priest, he knew it: they had a name for his kind—a whiskey priest, but every failure dropped out of sight and mind: somewhere they accumulated in secret—the nibble of his failures. One day they would choke up, he supposed, altogether the source of grace. Until then he carried on, with spells of fear, weariness, with a shamefaced lightness of heart.*

THIS MAKES ITS point: by the grace of God there is a "curious lightening of heart." Maybe the Bible *is* right! After all, it really boils down to redemption by faith alone. When the ideal works beyond a simple faith then that is something to rejoice about, but when more often it doesn't, then by faith we are saved from despair. He alone keeps us from the grave of the cynic and for that we should praise God all the more.

57

THIRD YEAR

A MIDDLE-CLASS SUBURBAN
housewife confronted the preacher with anger
in her voice and said, "Don't tell us everything we have
sacrificed for is no good!"

The guest preacher had done a pretty fair job of tearing
middle-class values apart. He had seriously challenged the
suburbanites' radical commitment to paying off the mortgage
and saving money in order to send the kids to college with
enough left over to retire on. He pointed out very articu-
lately that neither the New Testament nor the poverty of
the world seemed to justify that kind of blind dedication
and sacrifice.

Well! He got through to one woman at least!

Of course the preacher was right in principle (and I can
identify with what he is saying: One of the most liberating
experiences of my life was to sell my house), but what is
the whole truth? Would this young preacher be in the pulpit
at all if someone had not saved and sacrificed to put him
there? Would there ever be a permanent advancement in
education or knowledge or wisdom without men "squander-
ing" their time and energy to achieve these goals, neglecting
for a time the suffering in life? How have our great institutions of learning come about except through "indulgent"

men who were more willing to work to give to the greater good at the sacrifice of the immediate need?

So what is the real truth? I see as that preacher does what ought to be and I'm deeply disturbed by what is . . . but, *who*, just who in this world can stand up straight and tall and with the wisdom of God decide who is following the truth and who is not.

No! These are times, complex and gray. The truth is, more often than not, oversimplified (which is always an easy way of converting truth into fiction). There are few clear, neat, precise judgments to be made. And in fact, who is to decide the extent of our guilt when the judge is unable to divorce himself from the system that condemns us all?

JOHN SAID TO *[Jesus], "Teacher, we saw a man casting out demons in your name, and we forbade him, because he was not following us." But Jesus said, "Do not forbid him; for no one who does a mighty work in my name will be able soon after to speak evil of me. For he that is not against us is for us. For truly, I say to you, whoever gives you a cup of water to drink because you bear the name of Christ, will by no means lose his reward."* MARK 9:38-41 R.S.V.

IF THESE ARE complex and gray times, when it is difficult to make clear judgments, you would expect there would be a great deal more understanding and compromise. But like John's estimate of someone "who was not following us," we too are likely to be very quick to condemn those whose theological and social perspective is not the same as ours. Today most people, liberals very much included, are quick to make judgments about those "who are not following us" in word and action.

Judgment, criticism, and condemnation are some of the most alienating traits in the human condition. Today when things are the most difficult to understand and when clear choices are seldom available to us, we seem to be the most judgmental. The liberal who criticizes and talks incessantly about the apathetic, fence-sitting, uncommitted Christian is every bit the same as that stuffy, self-righteous, narrow, pious person who gossips about the moral condition of the young underdressed student in the next block.

Most, if not nearly all the time, we live in between truth and error. It is a fact of life that we seem to have a great tendency to ignore; we can seldom be absolutely sure of our choices and our actions. Most of the time we have to make a choice among several possible courses to follow, all of which have some element of error involved in them.

A young man who has broadened his thinking through military service comes home having learned to be very much appreciative of his black comrades at arms. He comes home, however, to very prejudiced parents. He has a choice. He can confront them with their prejudice, criticize them, shock them, and run the very real risk of alienation from them forever; or he can stay and try to help them to understand, running the risk of being tolerant of an evil for which there is no time left to be tolerant.

We in the church spend too much time talking about the exceptional and miraculous and we lose sight of the ordinary things of life. We are inclined to make the task of living sound too easy. Sermons are too smoothly closed with an easy solution that bids everyone to turn his needs over to Jesus and all will be well. We spend too much time telling about the inspirational moments and not enough on how to handle the much more frequent periods of confusion. We need a theology for life's gray areas.

When you read some of the magazine articles or books which describe a church that has been renewed or changed, you read all about the victories; nothing about the long periods of dryness and deadness and doubt. There are too many stories that deal with bright moments and not enough that take into account the overcast, fog-bound realities.

We see through a glass darkly. We need to know more about a God who seldom makes himself clear. We need a gray theology, not merely a gray (situational) ethic. Then perhaps we will be better able to learn how to live with ourselves when we are not so sure—which it is very essential to know how to do these days, it seems to me.

AUGUST

HOME FROM VACATION! Not a very good one; I was unable to relax and unwind. But I came home a little wiser than I went away and one can't help but admit that whenever that happens the experience has been worthwhile.

We had always heard how camping was the best way to

make friends. "Every camper is eager to be of help and is a paragon of cordiality"—so we heard. Well, we didn't experience this; somehow we were unable to find any friendly campfires.

Toward the end of our trip we pulled into a camp area outside Washington, D.C., and we were put in an overflow area which was nothing more than an asphalt parking lot. I was already tired, irritable, and hot, and all I needed to really complete the day was to get stuck out in the hot sun in a parking lot with no tables and no place to sit down. Well, of course, I became very unfriendly and I began to cuss out everyone from the National Park Service down to my youngest daughter who, much to my dismay, seemed to be enjoying our predicament immensely. I began to slam things around as I set up our tent. And mixed with varied invectives I started working on the camp stove to get supper going when the woman next to us, who had been quietly observing all this, looked over at me and said, "You sure go through hell having a good time, don't you?" I was stunned. She had hit the nail squarely on the head. This had been an unfriendly trip because *I* was having a hellishly good time. It was me all along.

But the thing that really disturbed me the more I reflected on my vacation personality was how fake I was. I was acting quite differently with strangers than I acted with people back home. Obviously I didn't need to impress these people with my charm, wit, and good manners since *they* were not the ones who paid my salary—besides I would never see *these* people again. I suddenly discovered that I was not treating people as persons so much out of my "deep and spontaneous" love for them as I was to create an image of myself as a sensitive and loving guy. I was appalled. I had seen something of myself that I didn't like. I was as much of a faker as the rest of the world.

Well, as I say, I learned something, and now I am back again involved in the life of the church. I'm not sure what I'm going to do about my discovery. Maybe I need to work harder at being myself. But, there again, maybe just being aware of my own deceptions is enough. Maybe this kind of awareness is how God recreates. I believe it is. We have to know something of what we are if we are going to be renewed in any significant way. Most especially, I know this: that God works in life like this—through an overcrowded camp area on a family vacation. He doesn't operate by allowing axe heads to float on water or causing the sun to stand still, but rather He recreates by using the events in a man's life in such a way that once in a while he sees himself or someone else in a much clearer and profound way. Whenever we are confronted with truth—whether it leads to ecstacy or judgment—it is a confrontation with God and one can only praise God for it no matter how threatening it is.

More often than not such a revelation is a "shaking of the foundations." Maybe this is what the Old Testament means when it says, ". . . for man shall not see me [God] and live" (Exodus 33:20). No one can face the total truth. God has to feed it to us bit by bit or we would never survive it. Come, Lord Jesus—but not all at once!

PETER DECLARED TO *him, "Though they all fall away because of you, I will never fall away." Jesus said to him, "Truly, I say to you, this very night, before the cock crows, you will deny me three times." Peter said to him, "Even if I must die with you, I will not deny you." And so said all the disciples.* MATTHEW 26:33-35 R.S.V.

NOW PETER WAS *sitting outside in the courtyard. And a maid came up to him, and said, "You also were with Jesus the Galilean." But he denied it before them all, saying, "I do not know what you mean." And when he went out to the porch, another maid saw him, and she said to the bystanders, "This man was with Jesus of Nazareth." And again he denied it with an oath, "I do not know the man." After a little while the bystanders came up and said to Peter, "Certainly you are also one of them, for your accent betrays you." Then he began to invoke a curse on himself and to swear, "I do not know the man." And immediately the cock crowed. And Peter remembered the saying of Jesus, "Before the cock crows, you will deny me three times." And he went out and wept bitterly.* MATTHEW 26:69-75 R.S.V.

IT SEEMS TO me (and I think Peter would agree) that these people who say "be yourself" had better be careful about what they are advocating. The advice to "know yourself" is a much wiser admonition.

The other day we were discussing a book on Christian ethics in one of our groups. The point the author seemed to be making was that our response (our actions) tell us what our commitment is. . . .

Some time ago I happened to witness a relatively minor automobile accident. A little sports car on a wet pavement was out of control and slammed into the side of a car coming in the other direction. A young girl, who had been driving the sports car, with blood running down her face from a cut on her forehead, was the first one out of the car. She ran around to the front of her MG, and looking horror-stricken at the smashed-up radiator, exclaimed with profound shock, "Oh, my car!" Conclusion: Her actions revealed that she is a cold, heartless materialist. She neither cares about other human life—those in the other car—nor does she care about herself. Her first love is the materialistic system that allows her to put cars, clothes, picture windows, country clubs, cocktail parties first, above everything else.

Now, of course, I don't know this girl at all. Possibly she is the cold, heartless, unconcerned person her statement in shock seems to imply. *But* it is also quite possible that she may be trying very hard *not* to be all those things. We can not conclude the worst about a person because of their spontaneous action in this or that situation. The driver of that car may very well be a selfish, worldly materialist, but she also may very well be aware of it and she may be trying very hard to do something about it. That, in fact, is what Christianity is all about—*becoming something you are not!* Half the battle is to recognize that your real self is corrupt and wants self-pleasure and glorification. The second half of the battle is to use your will coupled with the will of God *not* to be what you *know* you are.

It would seem to me the real conflict within oneself (and with the world) comes when one is not willing to admit what one's real self is like and rather *makes believe* that one is a genuinely good, righteous, loving person. It is the make-believe world that tears us up inside—not so much the corruption of the flesh that we tend to emphasize too much.

I have been rereading Hartman's *Holy Masquerade*. This

is the story of a struggle for truth and honesty which ends in insanity and suicide. But it was not the quest for truth so much as the denial of truth that resulted in tragedy. That is the point of the cross—it represents the denial of truth. This was the thing Jesus feared the most. He condemned hypocrisy over every other conceivable sin and he actually approved of the corrupt man who knew his own corruption (Luke 18:9-14).

The only thing that saves me is knowing this: that God loves the confessed sinner. (Peter was no exception. Hallelujah!) Otherwise, who could stand before God since every one of us *is* self-righteous? It is the recognition of that truth that sets us free to be something other than we are. The starting point in Christianity is this honesty about ourselves; the pilgrimage is to become more and more what we are not by the grace of God; the struggle is to know the difference between the will of God and our own selfish desires; and the victory is to discover freedom and joy underneath it all.

SEPTEMBER

"EVERY SUNDAY I go to church
I'm more upset when I leave than when I
get there, so I've stopped going. I have enough problems
all week. I look for a little comfort and a little assurance.

69

. . . I don't have to be reminded that the world is falling apart. Who needs it? I come to forget the front page of my newspaper for a while. . . ."

So said a woman who was obviously upset by our worship.

Which caused me to wonder, do we ever really *want* to hear the truth? (Presuming, of course, that the truth does break through on occasion, even from the pulpit.) Isn't the truth, nine times out of ten, upsetting rather than comforting? So don't we spend most of our lives avoiding it?

I'm sure that to one degree or another we contrive all sorts of devices to avoid the truth about ourselves. How much of our golf game and television football is an avoidance of confronting the reality of a shaky marriage or difficult children? Are not the possibilities of avoiding the truth actually endless: overwork; preoccupation with the church, town council, Elks club, front lawn, weekday television; losing oneself in booze, pills, pot; addiction to sports—golf, hunting, fishing, weekend football. Leslie Farber once said, "Ours is an addicted society." How many of us become "addicted" to avoid a painful truth about ourselves?

But this avoidance of confrontation is understandable: Confrontation is always painful. One of the advantages we Protestant "men of the cloth" have over those who are Roman Catholic is that most of us have built-in levelers— our wives. They sometimes have a marvelous knack of preventing us from harboring any illusions of grandeur about ourselves. They have an uncanny ability to speak the truth. A small illustration of what I mean:

I received a call from a woman who wanted to visit her daughter in the hospital. This particular hospital was a good hour's drive and she needed a ride. Could I take her?

Well, yes, I could; but I was reluctant. I was just about to go out with my wife Jo, and this was an inconvenient time. At any rate, Jo came along and we drove her to the hospital. As we arrived there was no convenient place to park. She asked me where the maternity ward was and I said I didn't know, but she could inquire at the desk. "You'll be all right," I said, "just ask at the desk." I let her out of the car in front of the entrance and drove off.

There was silence in the car for sometime after we drove away. Actually I was feeling pretty good. After all, I had sacrificed something. She had called me at an inconvenient time and I had given up my plans to run her down to the hospital.

After a few minutes my wife said, "You know you are very cold and selfish sometimes."

I was hurt. What she said was so contrary to my feelings of self-righteous well-being, I couldn't understand it.

I lashed back, "What do you mean?"

"Back there," she said, "dropping her off like that. You should have asked her if you could have taken her in. It's no wonder many people find it hard to warm up to you."

I was crushed. I didn't want to accept at all what she was saying. I, the loving, warm, person-centered, caring pastor, was hard to warm up to? I was hurt by the truth and we drove a long while before we spoke again.

PILATE SAID TO *him, "So you are a king?" Jesus answered, "You say that I am a king. For this I was born, and for this I have come into the world, to bear witness to the truth. Every one who is of the truth hears my voice." Pilate said to him, "What is truth?"* JOHN 18:37,38 R.S.V.

FOUR MEN CAME to the Lord and said, "Oh, Lord, tell us something that is true."

And so, to the first man, the Lord whispered: "No one knows the *complete truth* about anything—God, life, the universe, death. . . ."

"Oh, Lord, don't tell me that! You're upsetting me. I mean, how am I ever going to face this awful world if I don't have the truth about you. I need to know you're on *my* side. I need to know you're *mine*—especially *mine*."

And the Lord looked at him with sadness in his eyes and spoke to the second man with assurance in his voice, "This is true: We are responsible to one another."

"Oh, Lord, don't tell me that! Because I need to be free. I need to be free to do my own thing. I want to express myself and live. I want to find my own life and people hold me back. I have much to give the world and this one or that one keeps me from it by insisting I do this or that. Oh, Lord, I want to be free."

And the Lord looked with pity on him and said to the third man with compassion in his voice: "The truth is that a man never knows everything about himself."

"Oh, Lord, don't tell me that! I need to *know* myself. If I am to find happiness I must probe into the depths of my soul to search out my motives and illusions and dreams. I need to know myself and perfect myself before I'll be able to *do* anything. I mean, really do anything for anyone else. . . ."

And the Lord looked at him with a touch of impatience in his eyes and said to the fourth man: "The truth is there are no rules and regulations. The way to live life is simple. Love one another."

"Oh, Lord, don't tell me that because rules help me to be sure of my righteousness. Unless a man knows he is doing right, how shall he live? No, Lord, you are mistaken! Without the law we shall never be able to decide just who is right and who is wrong. After all, Lord, how will we be able to burn the tares which are among the wheat, if there is no way to tell the difference?"

If you looked very carefully you could see that the Lord's shoulders were somewhat rounded as he stood before them and tears began to glisten in the corners of his eyes.

The four men walked slowly away, but when they got out of earshot they huddled together to conspire against him.

OCTOBER

HAD A MEETING
with the school board over the
matter of released time in public schools.

The board, in order to get us to go away and not to go away mad, used painfully obvious flattery, and instead of our insisting that "flattery will get you nowhere," *we* got nowhere because we couldn't bring ourselves in the presence of all that ego to admit that their analysis of our needs was wrong. They said to us, in effect, that we are doing a good

73

enough job right now with our church education programs and we therefore don't need more time. Well, we certainly don't need more of *their* time.

It's odd, but I felt we were reaping what we have sowed for so many years. *We* have categorized religion by insisting it remain in a very special place. Now *they* are insisting that it stay there. We have neglected to show where Christianity is relevant to life. Now they say it is not. Now they say that kids need an education that will enable them to live and earn a living in the world and religion has very little if nothing to contribute to such a goal.

We have for so very long spoken weakly and now they speak strongly—saying, in effect, that "religion is very fine for women and children and we think everyone ought to be exposed to it but it has no place in the rough, cutthroat, nasty old world. So you're doing a fine job right now. Go back to your temples and stop trying to be something you're not. Stop trying to make yourselves more important than you are. Stick to your parades and dedications, your Sunday School classes, and your rituals, and we will deal with the important things like educating your children."

There was another important weakness in our armor. We were looking to protect our "establishments," our own personal interests, *just like they were.* Released time is passé. It never had much value aside from a token recognition by the school of the churches' existence and now it goes against the tide. Released time protects religious sectarianism. It protects our own point of view—and the school board knows it. And they were enjoying our awkward attempt at appearing ecumenical.

The only answer for us it so find a way of being effective

without insisting that the schools protect us from one another. It seems to me our only hope for being influential in education is to take advantage of the most obvious advantage we have over the public schools—an advantage which we have all so foolishly missed. The one thing we can do that they cannot do is to be more broad-minded than they are. They are paralyzed every time someone mentions religion and public schools in the same breath. We can be more open! In our schools we are free to mention *anything*—even God!

When we finally are able to really get together ecumenically, with no fears of exposing our own doctrinal positions, and when we finally learn to be open-minded, allowing ourselves to be freely confronted with the philosophies of the world, then, and not before, will we be influential. Then we will have some chance of being heard in the world. No one ever pays much attention to anyone who merely talks and never listens. In order to gain the ear of the world we have to learn to listen to all its doubts and philosophies and discoveries and to learn how to interpret the world in the light of the message of Jesus Christ. If we do that, then we will not have to go to the power centers of the world in order to get our job done—in order to protect our own self-interest.

STRENGTHEN THE WEAK *hands, and make firm the feeble knees. Say to those who are of a fearful heart,*
   "Be strong, fear not! Behold your God. . . .
                                                    ISAIAH 35:3,4 R.S.V.

HOW DO WE strengthen our weak hands and make firm our feeble knees? What has gone wrong? Somehow we have lost our authenticity. Has our integrity been lost because our chief concern has been our preoccupation with our own point of view, which is not what the world wants or needs or cares about? Is it possible that the world expects something else from us and has therefore been disappointed when we have not represented what it needs most? Could it be that what the world needs most and would most readily listen to from the church is the reaffirmation of the values that are spiritual?

Paul Tournier, a noted Christian physician, has said [*The Whole Person in a Broken World*, Harper & Row, New York, 1964] that today man outwardly embraces what is concrete and measurable and observable, but deep inside he has a thirst. He has a desire for love. He has a spiritual sort of loneliness. He continues to be haunted by the fear of death, the riddle of evil, and the mystery of God, and, while he no longer speaks about these things, they still haunt him. Today we need a new spiritual freedom and release. We need to somehow reassure people that what they yearn for deep down inside is legitimate and not imaginary. We have to reestablish the fact that man is not fully man until he is both physically *and* spiritually satisfied. Man is not whole and healthy man unless he can find expression for mind, body, and spirit.

One of the greatest experiences of my life has been to break out of the sterility of a technological world. I had trained myself well. I had carefully avoided the arts, the humanities, and the social sciences in order to spend time on what I considered the more worthwhile practical concerns of earning a living. So there was a whole world of knowledge which I neither understood nor knew existed.

But when I at last "came to myself" and for the first time looked at life and saw the tremendous significance and power of beauty, truth, goodness, and love, I was overwhelmed. It was like discovering something really new and important for the first time. I recognized that the great artists and poets and writers were really asking the questions that had all of a sudden become important to me too. Who am I? What is the meaning of life? What is the meaning of death? How do I find something worth giving my life for? Is there a meaningful place to stand in what seems to be a meaningless world? What are the essential values in life and why? These are spiritual questions, legitimate questions, *realistic* questions. These are questions for which technology has no proper answer. These are the questions that modern man has repressed, says Tournier. These are the questions that continue to gnaw at his insides and have caused his neurosis, his uncomfortableness, his sense of lostness. He is unable to face them because he's afraid there is no answer, so he represses them and he becomes sick inside.

The schools can do something about this as well as the churches. They can find ways of making these spiritual questions relevant and important. They can do a great deal toward promoting the arts. They can find ways of encouraging an interest in the real and incredibly important values of beauty, truth, goodness, and love. If we can encourage the schools to do this, then all the gimmicks like released time become of negligible value. This is what the church must encourage them to do— and this is our only legitimate relationship to the public schools.

OUR CLERGY GROUP met again.

An interesting and brief exchange took place. We were discussing O. Hobart Mowrer's book, *Crisis in Psychiatry and Religion*, and someone happened to mention that for Mowrer redemption comes to the sinner, or the guilt-ridden, when he himself atones for his sin. That is, through reconciling works a man slowly but surely moves from anxiety, repression, and indecision to confidence, inner strength, and joy. We are saved by works and not by faith alone!

Even though most of us would agree with Mowrer, it occurred to me that if this is so, then where does the mystical enter into the healing process? What of those sudden redeeming moments of inspiration and inner strength and peace? Do they have no healing value?

"Well," said one, "we all know that when someone comes to us to tell us they have had a spiritual experience that this person surely has psychological problems."

"That's a rather presumptuous generalization, isn't it?" demanded another.

"Well, there can be no doubt that there is a great deal about the psyche and spiritual matters that we know very little about," said someone else.

"Yes, but shouldn't we be sure about the spiritual? Isn't it our business to know something about the spirit?"

JESUS ANSWERED, "TRULY, *truly, I say to you, unless one is born of water and the Spirit, he cannot enter the kingdom of God. That which is born of the flesh is flesh, and that which is born of the Spirit is spirit.*" JOHN 3:5,6 R.S.V.

I WONDER SOMETIMES about the Spiritual power of God in one's life. Is it as mystical and forceful as we would like to make it out to be? We preachers talk a lot about it as something that is tangible and essential to the Christian life. Perhaps it is for some. . . .

I believe it was for me. In fact, I would go further to say that it is essential to anyone's healing, growth, and maturity.

There was a time when I would have seriously disagreed with this. Maturity was measured by your ability to stand on your own hind legs and outwit the opposition. It had to do with a certain pride in being alone and winning against a hostile world. Manhood was throwing dust into the eyes of others before they had the chance to swindle you. You had to work every moment to stay on top. The job, your success in business, the size of your house, the effect you had on important company, the impressions you made—these were the goals, these were the measures of maturity and success and manhood.

What changed my viewpoint? The same God who broke in on Abraham, Isaac, Jacob, Peter, Paul, Nicodemus, Augustine, Luther, Wesley, King—is it too presumptuous to believe that?

Do you have a better explanation? Can you explain how a dead, narrow, inarticulate, selfish man is opened up like a melon to think previously unthinkable thoughts, to reconsider long since rejected ideas, to take another look at values considered ridiculous, to set new goals never before considered? I'm not sure I understand it myself. It's even a little frightening because the Spirit asks a whole lot— more than I'm ever ready to give up, more than I'm ready

79

to let die in my life, more than I'm usually willing to do—like giving up the chance to enlarge my own identity by using and manipulating others, like letting die that little device I have of making myself feel better by finding a reason to act superior to others, like revealing what ought to be, so that what is becomes so unbearable that I have to do something about it. That is what the Spirit does to you—urging, suggesting, painting in a hundred images and forms ways to change, to grow, to mature . . . really mature and *become* beyond your wildest dreams. It is the Spirit that sets before you a special vision of tomorrow, beyond the horizon, a vision too often thought to be a laughable dream by the practical-minded, and then it is the Spirit that urges us on to discover again and again, in little ways, that the vision is true. That is the Spirit that breaks in on occasion and makes all things new.

The trouble is that the Spirit breaks in all too rarely and we, much too easily, slip back into self-reliance. The visions fade. We have the victory of Christ but we are too often without the victories. There are very, very few victories. There are too few experiencing the power of God—making the difference between a nice, nominal, respectable Christianity and a Christianity filled with a power that changes people and events. Where are the victories of the Spirit? I confess I am impatient. I want God to knock on a few doors and open a few eyes. Sometimes I feel like I'm beating myself to death on a wall of indifference. I know now that the ministry can be a very lonely business. It's not so much a loneliness coming from the lack of human affection as a loneliness because God often seems indifferent too. We are sometimes like men who are in a dark room groping for blind men to lead us to the light.

Ah, the Bible talks a lot about blindness. It's an excellent description of the human condition against which God's Spirit often seems so inadequate. The husband who can't see the spiritual warmth in his wife. The business man who believes he cannot be "ethical" and stay in business. The young person who is blinded by his total rebellion against anything he hears from the establishment. The "religious" person who is all wound up in a personal piety which colors his thoughts and actions a beautiful shade of respectability. The old guard who can't see that the revolution that is coming is inevitable and that in fact the whole Christian principle is based on change, and who fights change at every corner. Blindness! What an ideal word for our predicament. What a deadening, irresistible, stifling disease blindness can be. It must take every ounce of God's strength and patience to overcome it. I'm sure that's the message the cross brings to us. Even Jesus was up against it. In fact it killed him.

Yet somehow we trust in the power of His Spirit to even overcome the death caused by blindness. We trust because that's the victory. It's just a little hard to do sometimes because we live too close to the failures and disappointments.

Yet someone once said that in spite of disappointments and failures, "Even so we believe!"

And that's it after all, isn't it?

Therein lies the Spiritual power of God—in the simple act of believing. It's all in the believing because just by believing we are changed ever so little. Maybe it's hardly recognizable, but the change is there. And the one thing that's so important and different is that by believing, the chance is there; the eternal opportunity to be different from what we are—and that makes all the difference in the world!

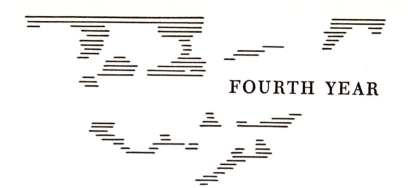

FOURTH YEAR

"ARENT THINGS JUST
awful today in the world?"

"Well, I don't know. Maybe they seem worse because we hear about what happens so quickly today. Years ago there could have been a catastrophe one hundred miles away and you would have never heard about it."

"Nonsense, things *are* worse today. All over the world there's trouble."

"Maybe you're right. But I guess part of the job is to try to make the world a better place to live in—rather than to worry about whether it's better or worse."

"The Christian's job is to go to church on Sunday and mind his own business. We have no right meddling in things that don't concern us."

"You don't think the world's problems should concern us?"

"No, I don't. We have enough problems of our own."

"You don't see any inconsistency between what we say we believe and indifference to people's needs?"

"Of course people have needs and we should take care of them. Why every year our church used to give out food all around the area here. We need to take care of our own, that's what I mean."

"Oh, then you think we shouldn't worry about thousands of Indians starving every day and about . . ."

"Of course it's too bad that all those people are suffering, but the trouble with them is that they want a handout. Let them work for what they get. I had to. Why Mrs. E and I came to this town fifty years ago and we had nothing. We worked hard to get what we have today. I'm sick of handing the world everything on a silver platter. No one ever did it for me. No one ever did it for this country when we needed it. If they need food in India let them grow it like we do. I say put them to work."

Just held this conversation with Mr. E. I am convinced that our generation is paying for this attitude today.

Over the news last night two scenes: a bunch of Mexicans isolated on a strip of high ground after a flood were interviewed by television cameras, and they spoke of losing everything; all they had left was food enough for two more days. Then the switch to New York and the opening of a bright, new, immense kitchen serving a hotel banquet hall with an amazing new oven where four thousand steaks could be cooked at one time. Most of us watch and see neither inconsistencies nor injustice, nor do we feel any shame nor any tears.

The horrible deadening narrowness and selfishness that is tragically unable to understand that some people are simply *unable* to meet the standards of the majority because of their circumstances, is one of the greatest threats to our society today. If a man is starving, why doesn't he get busy and grow some food for himself? If an unemployed man has no house to live in, why doesn't he get a job and rent himself a room? If a man is an alcoholic, why doesn't he use a little willpower and give up drinking? If a man is fighting with his wife why doesn't he kiss and make up? Apparently one of the most difficult things for some suburban people to understand is that some other people are unable to save themselves: there is no seed to grow, there is no job to get, there is no willpower left, there is no desire to make up.

Many people with this attitude are Christians. How terribly far removed we are from the Gospel. The Gospel is so inconsequential and meaningless to many Christians. But the Gospel has to matter for me. God! It's got to matter! His attitude reminded me all over again of what I have been running from all my life. I was brought up in the midst of this kind of parochial, selfish, self-reliant prejudice and I'd just heard it all over again. I think I can take anything but that. I can't survive if it doesn't matter to somebody. If there is no more to this ministry than playing the game, then I have really lost—it's all for nothing. The nice suburban showcase, the pure white pews, the carpeted lounge, the meaningless committees, the complacency, the protection of the establishment—My God!—we have two-legged "Keep Off the Grass" signs all over the place! And there is nothing more un-Christian than a "Keep Off the Grass" sign.

I pray to God that I can find the peace of God. I haven't found it yet. The peace I seek is knowing that *it matters* what I do. Is that too much to ask? Sometimes I can hardly bring myself to thinking about Sunday morning because of the deadening feeling that no matter what I say it will make no difference. I feel I'm talking about things that are so far from what people believe as to seem meaningless.

Besides, I'm finding it harder to relate the Gospel to myself anymore. Maybe that's the biggest problem. I'm drying up. I'm spiritually starving to death. I need the spiritual support of other people. I've got to hear other people pray like they mean it. Like it really matters to them. I've got to see some-one else get excited about God.

God give me a life that matters! May the Spirit yet break through in this church—and upon me.

"LET US HAVE *no imitation Christian love. Let us have a genuine break with evil and a real devotion to good. Let us have real warm affection for one another as between brothers, and a willingness to let the other man have the credit. Let us not allow slackness to spoil our work and let us keep the fires of the spirit burning . . ."*

ROMANS 12:9f PHILLIPS

THE TROUBLE WITH most of us is that we are spiritually starving to death. Oh, I don't mean that in the typically religious frame of reference. I mean that it's a case of allow-ing our own personal spirit to shrivel up and die.

For instance, take beauty: food for the spirit. How often do we get the chance to see the real beauty in people? When do we ever see that certain radiance in the skin and special shine in the eye and the smile? When do we ever worry about it in ourselves? When do we value it enough to want it?

For instance, take truth: food for the spirit. But how often do we get a chance to see the truth? Life is so full of incon-sistencies and little compromises. Little compromises that chip away at the soul. Inconsistencies that dry up any last puddles of the heart. But we are consoled, you know, because no one takes the truth too seriously. No one sees the connection between the two: Truth and beauty! Truth and spirit!

For instance, take goodness: food for the spirit. But goodness is a quality that's so elusive. "Why do you call me good?" Goodness, kindness, charity: what have they to do with the soul? But, on the other hand, goodness—generosity, unselfish affection—radiates and is somehow terribly attractive. If we are sometimes attracted by evil, how much more we are attracted by goodness. Or repelled by it! Whether we are attracted or repelled depends on our condition. Either way, goodness is a powerful ingredient. It's strong medicine.

How is it that we have lost the significance of these intangible things in life? How often have we taken a child by the hand and shown him a rose? How often have we sat down on a mountaintop and paid attention to the beauty of the earth? How often have we taken a minute to consider whether our mad dashing around has any foundation in truth or any clear ring of goodness?

The trouble is we've been brainwashed. The scientific world has washed out of our mind the sure truth of the intangible spirit of men. We feed the mind to make money, so we can feed our desires with things. *That* is tangible, real, touchable, undeniable truth. It's all in what you have and in what you have achieved. It's the analytically undeniable that is reality. Reality is no longer identified with truth, beauty, and goodness. These are intangibles. There are too many nutty people running around claiming that they possess these things for us to believe in the spiritual realities of life.

But we forget that we don't *possess* beauty or truth or

goodness. We can't ever seem to learn or when we do it's often too late or we have gone through too many years of desperation to know that we never possess them—rather they must possess us!

That's why they must be personified. God knew that. God knew that if the human spirit was to grow and mature, beauty, truth and goodness would have to be demonstrated concretely so that men might look at them and see them and love them. This is what he did in Jesus. He personalized them. Jesus is the way to spiritual abundance because he *is* truth, beauty, and goodness. If only we could learn how to encounter, see and love the spirit of Jesus, then, I am convinced, would come the new age. The most glorious age we can imagine. The new age where beauty is more obvious, where truth is more precious, where goodness is greatly to be admired. Then the spirit abounds and grows and *lives*. Then living comes alive.

Then life is abundant, indeed.

FEBRUARY

LAST WEEK WE were up in the
Vermont woods and what you feel up there
is almost indescribable. Those tall pine trees with their low-
est limbs forming a shelter over your head. The newly fallen
snow bending the branches down, and the snow itself, fall-

ing ever so gently and very vertically with not a breath of wind. And the quiet. The unbelievable quiet. You know we don't really know what quiet is: we live in an ocean of noise. But there in that place, in that moment you almost feel a part of the beauty and quiet and cleanness that surround you. You know, in that instant, that you somehow belong to it and at the same time you are beyond it. And you know there in the quiet that there is something more to this life than the rat race and the noise and the busyness. And suddenly you know that you belong to that something, whether it is the attraction of nature to Nature or of spirit to Spirit. You are not sure—but you guess that it is both.

So you come away from those woods a little different from when you went into them—ever so slightly different. You know you will never quite be the same again and you are glad because you have experienced something unexplainably profound about the very familiar. And the experience has somehow given you an assurance that the ordinary and simple and usual have something to do with the spirit, and even the incarnation is not quite as difficult to understand as it was before.

UP TO THE *present, we know, the whole created universe groans in all its parts as if in the pangs of childbirth. Not only so, but even we, to whom the Spirit is given as firstfruits of the harvest to come, are groaning inwardly while we wait for God to make us his sons and set our whole body free.* ROMANS 8:22,23 N.E.B.

A CERTAIN SENSE of freedom comes through when you are on the "mountaintop." You feel strong and ready for anything —even the valleys.

But, let's face it, it is not long before all the old anxieties and fears come back as you begin the descent. And when you lose what you had at the summit, you begin to wonder about its authenticity. Yet, if you are troubled by the loss of ecstasy, you have missed the point. Life is not ecstasy. Life is rather a continuing resurrection—a kind of ongoing and gradual liberation from our fears, anxieties, and valleys.

I would guess that the mountaintop helps you ever so slightly to become more courageous in the valleys. It provides a little more courage for what the Gospel demands: a kind of abandonment, a readiness to cast caution to the wind and to throw yourself into a course which you have been unable to follow because of your anxieties. It is to recognize all the old dangers of exposure to criticism, disapproval, and denunciation, and to cast them aside for something greater and of much more value, for something terribly important.

I imagine it is something like a battle cry. Like the soldier who is scared to death—with every nerve on edge, with sweat running down his back, with every sense almost aching and burning—who nonetheless runs toward the enemy taking risks his reason would not let him take, throwing his very life into the breach.

This is why reason seldom leads to commitment—or makes a good soldier. What man would fight if first he had to understand why? Wars are characterized by the inability to tell why. So it is with the first steps to personal freedom. Who can say why? Reason says, protect yourself. Be cautious. Make sure you've got the ability; make sure you don't turn people against you; make sure you've got the financial backing; make sure you won't be criticized.

This is why the whole created universe groans: *We don't want to take the risk.* This is why God wrestles with Jacob and hounds Jeremiah and pleads with Peter. Sometimes God kicks us out the door of our warm, comfortable rooms; still we resist, and we groan and complain and drag our feet rather than face the consequences of the battle.

Even the Vermont woods say you are a part of nature, of natural circumstances. You belong to the quiet and the beautiful and the sweetness of life. But also you don't belong to the quiet, to this place. You are awakened enough so that you know that there is more than the natural alone. You know you cannot really stay there; that this kind of peace is only temporary; that the sense of contentment is momentary at best. And you are urged to go beyond it and *through* it. Behind it all there is something so very much more, something very much worth having.

And so you take the risk and you reach out for more. By some miracle of courage you lay yourself open a little more. Not merely to take the risk of being wounded in battle, but also the risk of *not* being wounded. You risk asking questions that echo out against emptiness that are unanswerable. You expose yourself to the possibility of emptiness, to the deadening, discouraging, and stifling apathy and complacency and indifference of the world around you. There is nothing more painful than to be passionately involved, to be on fire, to dare everything—only to discover that for some incredible reason your fire burns alone.

But you take that risk nonetheless because dedication to the sweetness of life is death in disguise. That mysterious something insists you go on. It drives you toward itself, and you continue because there are no alternatives worth considering. And you *want* to go on: you want to continue because you have tasted a new ingredient in life. You discover a certain kind of freedom, a new kind of self-expression, an indescribable attraction to something which is far more precious than life itself.

_____ JUNE _____

"WHY SHOULD I join a church?

After going to this class every week for two years, I don't know if I should join this church or not. I'm confused."

"I'm not sure what I'm supposed to believe as a Christian. Maybe it's just that membership seems so unimportant. Isn't it more important what you feel about things? I'm not going to feel any different after I join than before, so what's the use?"

"Yes, you know, I agree; the church wastes so much time on its organizations and its buildings and. . . . well, whatever they do in all those committee meetings. Who needs it? Why can't we just be Christians where we are?"

"Most people who I see around here are stiff . . . formal. You know what I mean? They're sort of up-tight. You said Jesus gives us freedom; well, I don't see much freedom.

Wasn't it somewhere in the Book of Acts where a bunch of early Christians were really swinging. . . . I mean, weren't they accused of being drunk or something? Man, nobody could accuse us of that around here!"

"Church is what you feel and what you do. What you believe in doesn't matter much. Churches and preachers are always talking about what you're suppose to believe in. I'm not sure I believe in any of it! So why should I join?"

These comments were heard during the last few sessions of classes preparing our youth for membership in the church. For two years we had met together and now we were approaching Pentecost Sunday when they would all very dutifully go through the motions of joining the church. Now, however, all the work done to free these kids up to the point of honest confrontation was beginning to have its effects. They were being honest and I was squirming a bit. They were making some pretty basic observations . . . and I was feeling some twinges of pain, thinking that it would be very difficult to refute their accusations, to alter their feelings.

Then one young woman said, "I suppose you are right. I don't know for sure what to believe in. I mean, who understands all this stuff about the trinity, virgin birth, resurrection from the dead . . . but understanding all that is not important if you have found something that I'm not sure I can describe to you. But just listen for a minute. When I first came to this church I didn't know anybody and now I think I've found something; it's sort of a feeling, a feeling that I belong, a feeling, well, that people care what happens to me and are even willing to accept me as I am. When Mrs. K put her arms around me and kissed me and said she loved me, *that* was worth something; and when I was scared and worried about N being sick, I came to Fellowship and I felt like you all understood and it was real and I felt your warmth and spirit and your love. And I've been thinking, is that the church? Isn't that the church, belonging like that? I want that very much so I guess that's sort of why I'm joining."

Beautiful words, but is she right? Young people keep saying, why do we have to put up with the organization? And sometimes I think they are right.

JOHN CAME, AND *he fasted and drank no wine, and everyone said, "He is a madman!" The Son of Man came, and he ate and drank, and everyone said, "Look at this man! He is a glutton and wine-drinker, and he is a friend of tax collectors and outcasts!" God's wisdom, however, is shown to be true by its results.*   MATTHEW 11:18,19 A.B.S.

I FEEL IT's like Jesus said: if we play it real straight, un-emotional, austere, judgmental, critical, with a frowning disapproval, there are those who will justly say we are madmen. "Who are they to be acting so superior and self-righteous and cold!"

But even so, if we play it too free and loose, if we allow ourselves to become a free, swinging, open sort of group, then some people will say we are acting like drunkards, fools, and they will be fearful because there will be too much emotion and too little restraint.

But why does it always have to be one or the other? The kids are right—we need more freedom. We adults, for the most part, are up-tight and we feel uncomfortable when the party swings too freely. And yet the adults are right too—there needs to be responsibility, organization, and straight thinking. Life is not a party.

What those kids were saying about "feeling" their Christianity was beautiful. I, too, need to "feel" it. I need to know somehow that this is a kind of family that I belong to and that I'm one of the brothers. I need to know that I'm accepted and that there are those who will throw their arms around me and allow me to throw my arms around them—crying or laughing, either one.

Why are we so afraid of feeling it? Can we ever be open enough to appreciate people if we don't feel our Christianity down deep in the center of our being? If we don't feel anything then what will we be looking for in people? We will be checking out their intelligence, the way they operate at a social affair, what they have accomplished, where they live, the goods they've accumulated. If we don't feel, won't we miss much of the real person in people? If we don't feel, won't we miss or overlook or even become intolerant of the inability of some people to respond or grow or mature? Won't we tend to use the wrong yardstick for our mental measurement of people? Don't we have to feel something of someone's lonely fear of revealing too much of himself in order to understand his reluctance to enter a discussion group? Don't we have to feel for someone who is simply not prone to reading and studying and philosophizing over this issue or that? Don't we have to feel for someone who is not an activist, but whose simple faith shows in her warmth for her husband or son or daughter? Don't we have to really feel some of the same anxieties and tensions that other people do in order to become anywhere near able to love, to care about, to belong, to be trusted by one another? Don't we have to be ready to cry with those who cry, rejoice with those who rejoice in order to be a part of a Christianity that is deep and loving and real? Why are we so afraid to feel?

As an alternative to "feeling it," we build organizations. We reduce our religion to logical (or illogical) propositions and doctrines and put it in a can with a label on it that identifies the contents as something we call Christianity. And those that don't have all the adult white hang-ups about emotion and personal exposure and making a fool of oneself, such as the young and the disaffected blacks, say, "Your Christianity is unreal and I'm not sure I fit in."

We do not dare to miss the humanity in people and in ourselves. I believe that is the universality of Christ. I believe that is what Jesus meant when He said no one got to the Father but through him. He meant that access to God had to do with the loving, compassionate, truthful, joyful Spirit that He revealed and personified. I believe that Paul's expression "to be in Christ" means to be somehow led by that Spirit. It means that there is a certain very universal Spirit that is or can be a part of us and that Spirit is connected with God. That Spirit leads us to God. It is a Spirit that is best and most completely identified in the man from Nazareth and it has to do with becoming more human, more sensitive, more genuine, more open, more liberated. It's available, this Spirit! It's recognizable. Some who claim Christ as Lord do not have it. Others who never heard of him very much have it. It forms an unspoken fellowship that goes beyond barriers of race or language or culture. It's magnetic, attractive, "real," and most of all it has the power of God.

Lord, we need to *feel* this Spirit. We need to be grasped by it and changed. Those of us who are all bound up in proprieties and respectabilities and logical analysis, all of us who are so very practical—*we* need that Spirit!
Come, Lord Jesus!

*   *   *
          *   *
     * *   *
   *   *   *
*   *   *
      *   *

*   DECEMBER

"HELLO, PASTOR?"
"Yes."

"This is Mrs. N. How are you? You know we must get down to see you some Sunday morning. Harold has been so busy traveling all over the place and we've bought a new house you know. Probably shouldn't have done it, it's so much work. It seems every weekend this or that needs fixing. There's so much lawn to take care of . . . seems like you just never finish working. Harold is always so exhausted . . . day and night he just keeps going all the time. Say, did you know our baby is just three weeks old today!

"Which brings me around to what I called about: are you planning a baptism soon? Maybe I make too much of it, but I just don't like to wait too long to have little Harold baptized."

"Tell me, Mrs. N, are you a member of this church? You know it's been so long I don't recall and in order for me to baptize the baby either you or your husband has to be a member of a Christian Church."

"Well, no, we're not members of your church. Just seems every time you have new people join, Harold is on a trip somewhere. But I was brought up in the Reformed Church. I was confirmed by Pastor K . . . wonderful man."

"Oh, I didn't know about your Reformed Church background. Well, then you probably know something about our baptism procedures. . . . "

"Well, not really, it's been so long and little Harold is our first, you know."

"Then could you and Harold come by the church. . . say, some evening this week. I would like to explain a little about baptism and answer your questions about it. You know, there are so many different versions of baptism. . . . "

"Questions? Oh, I don't think we would have any questions. You just tell us when to be there and we'll be sure to make it."

"But there are questions I must ask you during the baptism ceremony, and if you have any reservation about answering affirmatively to any of them it would be best to review them beforehand."

"Now, pastor, just don't you worry about the questions. You just set the date. By the way, would it be too much to ask if you could give us a couple of Sundays to shoot for? As I say, Harold travels so much. . . . "

TO ANOTHER HE *said, "Follow me." But he said, "Lord, let me first go and bury my father." But he said to him, "Leave the dead to bury their own dead; but as for you, go and proclaim the kingdom of God." Another said, "I will follow*

100

you, Lord; but let me first say farewell to those at my
home." Jesus said to him, "No one who puts his hand to the
plow and looks back is fit for the kingdom of God."
LUKE 9:59-62 R.S.V.

" 'I KNOW YOUR works: you are neither cold nor hot. Would
that you were cold or hot! So, because you are lukewarm,
and neither cold nor hot, I will spew you out of my
mouth.' " REVELATION 3:15,16 R.S.V.

NOT AN UNUSUAL conversation at all. And I must confess after
insisting that this couple hear the questions and explanations
about baptism, I end up doing it for them and then I usually
never see them again until the next child is born.

Maybe this is one of the things about the suburban
church that is hurting it the most. Maybe out of its sincere
effort to be loving, out of its desire to never reject anyone or
say an unkind word or get angry or judgmental, that loving
has become unreal. It has become lukewarm. It has lacked
integrity and is therefore meaningless. We are reluctant to
tell it like it is, for fear that we will alienate too many
people and lose the battle of the mortgage. We can't afford
to tell Mrs. N that we feel baptism is a big step for any
parents to take, that it requires a commitment to bringing
up the child in the Christian faith, and in order for a parent
to do that there must be a rather persistent involvement
with other Christian people who are also searching for a
sense of the presence of God in their work and worship.

Can we do that as a church? Can we start insisting that
we mean what we do? What would happen if we took

baptism, confirmation, marriage, the funeral very seriously —not performing these functions unless they are thoroughly understood, unless there is some sort of commitment made.

If we do people will not understand. People will assume we are being self-righteous, judgmental, and pietistic. We will run the risk of becoming all those things that have created narrow-minded, egocentric, prejudiced churches and denominations. We run the risk of placing ourselves above people, as their judges, somehow determining whether they are sincere enough, or willing enough, or whether they meet *our* standards of Christianity or not. It becomes the same old struggle between acceptance and integrity. How do you accept the sinner without becoming a part of the sin? How do you say I love you without saying I agree with you? How do you say I don't like what you're doing but let's be friends?

Is the answer to accept *any* standard? Is the answer to say, "It doesn't matter how you live or what you believe, come and join us?" That sort of invitation, said or implied, is terribly destructive.

Take a high-school girl who can not be controlled by either her mother or father, who has violent and vicious arguments with them both. What is the problem? Is it too much authority? Are the parents being oppressive tyrants? Not in this case at least; although I suppose excessive restraint could have produced similar responses. But after lengthy discussion it appears that the daughter is utterly convinced her mother doesn't care about her or love her at all. Why? Because there are absolutely no standards, no restraints, no rules to live by. "My mother doesn't care what time I'm home at night, who I'm going out with, or where

I'll be, she's a *nothing* when it comes to being a mother and I hate her."

Perhaps we are awakening to the discovery that we are a "nothing" when it comes to being a church. True, no one hates us but that too is a sign that we haven't done anything to arouse such a genuine emotion. Much of the time we stand for "nothing," and without the family dynamics that that young girl was involved in, we are simply ignored, we are not to be taken seriously.

And so precisely because we seldom arouse anyone's anger, and because we never ask any embarrassing questions, and because we believe in an "inherited" Christianity, and because we avoid the controversy at any cost, we never change. We never grow. We are never able to become mature enough persons to take on any real mission in our society. Worst of all we never learn how to love and therefore miss out on real living.

The problem with most churches is that we have tried to be loving by avoiding the pain that real loving brings. We have sacrified integrity for budget, principle for filled pews on Sunday morning, honesty for a surface sort of peace. We have avoided the struggle. We have not really offered people something to believe in, something they can grab hold of and use as a principle and cause for living. We have not been honest with each other and have avoided the controversy and confrontation at any cost. And so we have not suffered enough. The power in the black struggle for justice is that they have suffered, which is the force behind any great cause: from early Christianity to the American Revolution to the six-day Israel-Arab war to black power—the key to power behind a cause is suffering.

103

Is there any other way to manhood, fulfillment, peace that does not include struggle, disappointment, suffering, and sacrifice? I do not believe there is. Granted struggle and trials do not always bring maturity; they also destroy, embitter, and dehumanize. This is the great mystery of creation, but we cannot look at those who are hurt by the struggle and say, "What an accursed creation this is to cause so much misery." Rather let us say, "What can we do to help people meet the struggle and achieve fulfillment and even peace?"—and maybe in the very process achieve these things ourselves. Maybe in the long run, we can do nothing meaningful without agonizing over our prejudices, our principles, our performance in this world. Without that agonizing, there is no urge to change or become something more than we are. If you were designing the universe, how would you do it any different? How indeed would you achieve maturity without the pain?

FIFTH YEAR

_____MARCH_____

MET J AGAIN today. He's one
of those clergyman who would sing freedom
songs at the old ladies' home. I have the deepest respect for
J. He is very courageous. He is very sure of what is right
and wrong. He speaks without compromising himself one
bit by the situation he finds himself in . . . as I say, he is one
who would talk about radical protest to a man who was
about to undergo radical surgery.

But I admire him because he is both courageous and
crystal clear about his convictions, and I am not privileged
to have either of those virtues. It must be something of a
luxury to be utterly sure of what you believe and have the
courage to act on it no matter what.

Somewhere I read that those who see things as clear-cut,
in an either/or fashion, are the doers. They are the ones who
change things. Those who see things as complex, who see all
the many facets of the argument, are the ones who seldom
do much at all. I would hate to place myself among the
latter, but as much as I dislike "Rock of Ages" I still sometimes find myself chirping along with those who are unable
to sing otherwise.

AND [JESUS] WENT *on from there, and entered their synagogue. And behold, there was a man with a withered hand.*

107

And they asked him, "Is it lawful to heal on the sabbath?" so that they might accuse him. He said to them, "What man of you, if he has one sheep and it falls into a pit on the sabbath, will not lay hold of it and lift it out? Of how much more value is a man than a sheep! So it is lawful to do good on the sabbath. Then he said to the man, "Stretch out your hand." And the man stretched it out, and it was restored, whole like the other. But the Pharisees went out and took counsel against him, how to destroy him.

MATTHEW 12:9-14 R.S.V.

CAN'T YOU PICTURE it? Jesus in church some Sunday morning, disrupting services with all sorts of dramatic gestures, upsetting the traditional patterns. Would Jesus have taken part in chancel drama? Modern dance in the aisles? Rock group in the balcony? Surely, he was partial to the dramatic. He said very dramatic things. He used stories to make his points. He disrupted traditions to teach a truth. Jesus used the shock technique with great impact and effectiveness. He upset many people.

So does J. J does not hesitate to upset people nor does he hesitate to disrupt the traditional forms. J is never reluctant about telling it like it is. But J is not Jesus.

I suppose it may be a part of my own defense mechanism to say that J would have to be Jesus in order to be as sure as he is about what he is saying and doing. Maybe it's just that I could never picture myself being that sure, so I need an excuse. But recognizing that as a possibility does not alter the difficulty in determining just how to change attitudes and points of view. Do you do it forcefully with a stick or with careful urging, building confidence, loving and caring?

How do you help people across that threshold of personal change? How will many people transform their value system and overcome their prejudices? How will some of them ever see the vital and often thrilling connection between the events of the Bible and the issues today? How will they understand that the *essential* elements of Christianity have to do with the very fabric of life and that to ignore them is to ignore one's own existence?

Take the issue of justice for the oppressed people in our land: did not God say to the authorities of Israel something about real love requiring real justice? How do you bring people to the point where they see the connection between love and justice?

Take the beautiful optimism that many young people have today, that out of the ashes will come a new earth. They have a poetry all their own about the possibilities of a new world. A poetry not unlike Isaiah 35 or Revelation 21! How do you help people capture a piece of that vision for themselves?

Take the moving, dynamic story of redemption from Abraham to Paul: God's own vital, often destructive, sometimes violent struggle with his world in order to bring about salvation; that is, to rescue His world from greed, ignorance, poverty, hate, bigotry—indeed, all the life-destroying forces. Is that process of redemption happening today? How do you help people to see that redemption is a not-so-simple struggle involving their very lives?

Take the idea of God's demand that somehow we change and like Abraham move out seeking the promised land— a new land, a new earth. Or the idea that like Paul, we need a personal transformation in order to receive enough of the new vision to even have the courage to take the risks that *this* kind of emergence involves. Isn't this the struggle going on today between those who would remain where they are and those who have caught the vision of a new earth and are trying to move out? Today there are those who can not accept the system any longer as it is: all the shady business deals; a government speaking out against violence, but at the same time using it as an instrument of its own in the world; the vast area of society with double standards, demanding of their young people that they must not lie or act dishonestly, while they cannot face the truth about themselves—denying their own racism, building ABM's in the name of freedom but cutting down on aid to education and welfare, going to the moon before giving farm workers the same rights as auto workers or bus drivers. Isn't this struggle the Biblical story? How do you help people see that to escape our own sin requires a revolution within one's own heart as well as in the heart of our society? How will people see the need for God's disciples to lead the way toward a new heaven and a new earth?

I would convince people of all this by beating them over the head with it. But recognizing the danger of rationalizations, I would have to say very emphatically, that is not the way! The way is not judgment, shock, coercion. No one ever became aware of the excitement nor discovered that deep down feeling within of being caught up in a cause or purpose beyond oneself by being shamed or embarrassed or threatened or cursed. No one ever learned how to love by force. Even God has demonstrated that fact to us. He does not *force* us to love him. He shows us the way, the beauty, the truth, the incredible love of God; but he never forces us to accept it. He never seeks to destroy our humanity or our freedom to choose against his route. God is ready to move the stars in the heavens, change the whole course of human history, allow nations to destroy, and greedy men to rule before he is willing to force his love on us. God knows that a forced love is not love at all because real love must be voluntarily given or it is composed of ulterior motives and underlying purposes and encourages only distrust. One must build, tediously, brick by brick, stone by stone, nail by nail. One must prove his trustworthiness, his honesty, his kindness, his compassion, his love. Yes, one must love anyone he hopes will change or there will never be a change. Love is a prerequisite. One cannot change another much by hate or anger or viciousness or insult or force—one must just love.

Eric Fromm has said, "Unlike force, [love] requires patience, inner effort and, most of all, courage. To choose to solve a problem by love requires the courage to stand the frustration, to remain patient in spite of setbacks. It requires real potency, rather than its perverted facsimile: force." It may be that by this definition the solution of love may be beyond me. It may be that I cannot contain my anger and impatience, and just possibly the hurts and disappointments and failures may accumulate to the point of despair. It may very well be that my courage to stand the frustration will not be enough, but here I stand committed to the way of love. Many will argue that that way is too slow. We are in a revolution, we are in a crisis situation, we need to burn the place down, then people will listen. There is no time for careful urging. No! The way of love mustn't be confused with weakness or sentimentality. The way of love requires truth

111

and justice and leads to a cross. That is why the way of love requires a revolution of the kind that does not set fires to buildings but sets fire to the human heart and changes values and points of view.

I am utterly convinced that J's way merely polarizes people. People line up on the side they were already on to start with, and very little real change takes place. After all, even Jesus had to take it all on himself. He had to vicariously love those who he sought to change, and that's the way it is—like it or not!

NOVEMBER

"I FEEL so guilty. I mean I don't have the time. I keep asking myself over and over if it's right for me to spend so much time at the office. And you don't help matters any when you ask me to work on this project or that committee. I just don't know. What are the guidelines for deciding how much time you should spend with your family, yourself, your church, your community and your job?"

So says a successful, well-meaning executive wrestling with his predicament. What do I say to him? Do I continue to pressure him into working for the church, which of course cuts into his already inadequate time at home? Hardly! But how will this man keep in touch with the real

Christ if it isn't convenient and practical for him to do so in his leisure time? The trouble is, leisure time is a myth in this community. Leisure time is a working-class benefit. The executive types are jetting to Europe, California, Texas, Chicago, and are gone for weeks and months at a time. Many are strangers at home. Does the church have any right to make them "stranger" yet?

Which, of course, brings to mind the question of what the basic shape of the church should be like. Maybe the neighborhod church is passé. Maybe we're structured wrong. Maybe the church needs to become something more than a leisure-time organization. Maybe, for instance, we need more "worker priests." Maybe we ought to be training people who are already trained to make a living. We need more occupational ministries. We need to put ministers on the jet plane and in the office instead of leaving them home with the women and kids.

Of course the women and kids need ministering to also. Especially since Dad is jetting all over creation. But I need a masculine faith. I don't like the idea of being left home with the women and children while everyone goes off to war in the city. It somehow offends my masculinity! I can't help feel that I could do so much more with a slide rule in my hand than I can in the conventional church structure. My greatest joy is conversation with the thinking non-believer, a chance I seldom get in the parish.

Yet at the same time there is something that convinces me I'm in the right place. The longer I am here the more I am sure that this is where I ought to be in spite of the frustrations presented by structures and time. And after all, it takes time for any of us to reach the point where our values change enough so that the real purpose of our living begins to emerge. It takes time for a man to discover that there is no line to be drawn between work and worship. And maybe it will take more time before the church discovers how to stop demanding that he spend time supporting the organization rather than helping him to learn how to apply a practical faith to his living and working.

How you do this within the present structure I don't know. Just the fact that I am dependent on his supporting an organization that is, for him, quite meaningless and only causes him frustration, is one of the biggest obstacles to change that I know, because if I sacrifice the structure I sacrifice my own security. Sometimes I think that all these books in which I read about churches that have come alive in various ways are hardly believable. Where indeed are these people who have seen the light? Is it even possible the way we are organized? That's a question only time, patience, prayer, experience, and a great deal of wisdom will answer. Lead on, Oh Lord!

BUT SOME MEN *came down from Judea and were teaching the brethren, "Unless you are circumcised according to the custom of Moses, you cannot be saved." And when Paul and Barnabas had no small dissension and debate with them, Paul and Barnabas and some of the others were appointed to go up to Jerusalem to the apostles and the elders about this question. So, being sent on their way by the church, they passed through both Phoenicia and Samaria, reporting the conversion of the Gentiles, and they gave great joy to all the brethren. When they came to Jerusalem, they were welcomed by the church and the apostles and the elders, and they declared all that God had done with them. But some believers who belonged to the party of the Pharisees rose up, and said, "It is necessary to circumcise them, and to charge them to keep the law of Moses."*   ACTS 15:1-5 R.S.V.

Here there cannot be Greek and Jew, circumcised and uncircumcised, barbarian, Scythian, slave, free man, but Christ is all, and in all.   COLOSSIANS 3:11 R.S.V.

EVEN IN THE early church there was disagreement and frustration about how the church was to be organized. Some would say we need a church for both the circumcised (people concerned and occupied with existing church structures) and for the uncircumcised (people not interested in the organized church, but occupied with secular vocations and issues). What is needed most, however, is a sense of commonness regardless of structure, tradition, or place of business. This underlying sense of belonging together without a binding structure is what seems to be emerging out of our present parish experience.

It really begins with the realization that our real ministry to the world is here in our community and not in some remote region of glory as dramatic missionaries on some hostile frontier. A while back our denomination was promoting the pairing of city and suburban churches. This was a grand opportunity for us to go to the inner city and devote our time to the ghetto community and of course for them to come here and do the same. But we soon realized how impossible this was. It was impossible because of the stark-naked reality that we have no one in our congregation who is motivated enough to go, probably because no one is directly affected by inner-city conditions. After all, we don't even care enough for our own elderly, widows, etc., so how and why are we going to do for strangers what we will not even do for our own?

What is the way to motivate people? To put it bluntly, the only way people are motivated is when the problem directly concerns their own welfare, unless, of course, there are some very highly committed and stable persons around. No! I am convinced that our mission is *not* in South Nairobi, Kenya, nor is it in downtown Newark, nor is it in East Granville Corners, Nebraska. It's here right where our church finds itself: let's not deceive ourselves for another minute about it.

It's here because the motivation is here. Our people are directly affected by such problems as drugs, alcoholism, mental health, care of the elderly, juvenile crime and vandalism, incompetence in government, racism. They are affected, so therefore, it is easier to find social ministries at the point where life hurts the most.

But also it's here because otherwise there would be a sort of superficiality about it all. We would be one of those missionaries who on a regular basis conveniently leaves the scene of the crime—who works in the city and lives in the suburb—and there is something hypocritical about that. Also, there is a need for "toe-to-toe ministries." That is, we have simply got to learn how to love the person whom we cannot escape from if we are ever going to learn how to really love the stranger. It's quite often easier to love a stranger than a member of your own family. You don't have to live, sleep, and eat with a stranger—for a time you can always be especially loving. It is often the most difficult test of faith to love and care for the guy who is bleeding all over

116

you every day—especially when you're not able to stop the bleeding. We have to learn how to love right here *where there is no escaping the consequence of loving.*

But our mission is here also because we know better what we are doing here. We can relate to those who share our condition. We can understand what it means to work eight or ten hours a day and in addition spend two or three hours commuting to and from work. We can understand the frustrations of the bored suburban housewife whose life is centered around the mundane routines of dishes and diapers and douches. We can understand the teenager who being saturated with "things" looks elsewhere for his kicks. We can understand the pressures to conform to a value system that admires the cocktail personality and backyard barbecue fortresses. We can understand the prestige of owning a lawnmower you can sit on and a green grass lawn complete with picture window you can sit behind. We can understand these things because we are a part of them: they are our problems. Where else are we going to better discover how Christ relates to life than right where we live it the most?

But this leads to a further consideration for suburbia. The ministry here has got to be an ecumenical one. If our mission is in the community—this community—then this automatically rules out denominational ties *because the only denominational cooperation to be had is across community lines.* We simply must learn how to cooperate inter-denominationally within the communities where we find ourselves. We simply cannot deal with the real issues denominationally because this fragments our efforts. Each community is unique. Each community has its peculiar problems and needs; therefore, denominations cannot possibly generalize about the form the

117

local church's mission must take—only those churches which are actually *involved* can intelligently plan the form of mission for their community.

Whenever there is ecumenical cooperation on a local level about some local problem there is power, authority, prestige, and resources, which no single congregation could ever assemble. Obviously local power structures will be far more anxious to listen to someone who represents *all* the churches in town than they will be to someone who speaks for the Reformed Church on Main Street. Obviously, when six or seven churches band together on a given problem it will be far easier for them to find the financial backing necessary to do the job. Obviously, when several churches are cooperating their resources are vastly expanded. There are many more diversified boards, agencies, and resource people to call on along with the real advantage of being able to gather more of the best kind of people in the community to do the job.

In our particular situation this kind of ecumenical cooperation has been highly successful because of the openness and willingness of the local clergy to spend time and effort on community problems and needs. So many projects have been tried they are almost too numerous to name; a Community Counseling Service; Fish, an emergency volunteer service to the community; Days of Encounter, days when high school youth of all denominations are free to come to discuss, sing, talk, experiment, and experience together; Inter-church School classes for retarded children; Choral Festival with music from different traditions; Human Relations Council; a Center for stimulating discussion of mutual concerns between secular local power groups; Adult

Ecumenical School—to name some of our ecumenical projects over the years. Of course, these have met with varied success; some are no longer being done, others are continuing. But these at least represent the kind of cooperative ventures possible *only* through ecumenical action. No single church has the resources to achieve such goals. My hat is off to our local congregations and clergy for their creative fellowship and ideas. This has been one of the most stimulating aspects of my ministry in Park Ridge.

But, in spite of all this, I am convinced *ecumenism does not mean church merger* either denominationally or locally. I do not say this because I believe we have a particular heritage or doctrinal tradition to protect. But merger at the top, on a national denominational basis, is rather futile since few at the grass-roots level care very much anymore about the name on the sign above the church door. It is what is inside the door that counts and vast, grand mergers do not significantly change that.

But neither is merger on the local level very meaningful either. Local merger seldom solves anything. Quite the contrary, it rather makes the problems we all have greater in magnitude. One gets weary enough worrying about the quality of our own Christian Education without merging with another local church that has similar if not worse problems in their church school. Bigger churches seldom solve anything, and in part may make it more difficult because of the greater remoteness of core people.

Ecumenism is rather an "underground" merger. It has to do with cooperating Christians working out their common concerns for the problems of their mutual community together, motivated by their own particular fellowship under

Jesus Christ. There is a common church. A brotherhood that requires no structure or organization other than the simple fact that we experience Christ's Spirit in and through another's concern and actions. Many times I have felt a genuine bond in Christian brotherhood with some Roman Catholics as well as with some from other Protestant denominations; and it comes through our actions together. There is an unspoken, shared Christ speaking to us in powerful and intimate ways. That I believe is as Jesus himself would have it.

The form of the local church must center on local issues and it must be ecumenical. I suppose only God will be able to see to it that this happens. There often is just too much power, pride, and authority to be overcome to let it happen too easily, but then that is the challenge and maybe that is challenge enough to bind us together.

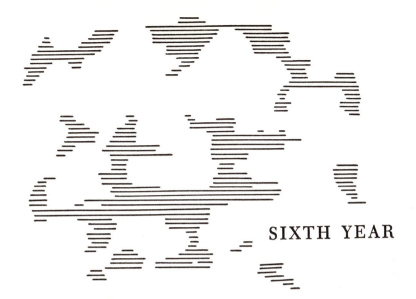

SIXTH YEAR

A FEW HAVE gathered to
concern themselves with renewal in the
church. So far we have met with only frustration and dissension. There are nine of us and we can't agree on what to do.

The problem is this: we don't want to get too personal with this religion business. We are afraid of threatening people too much.

We don't want to face the fact that the Gospel *is* threatening. It is a call to change in a radical way. It requires the old person to die, to really die—or it's no good. It involves a real conversion (or perhaps "inversion" is a better word) of our value system and priorities. It means a change in people's attitudes or we are not going to change the character of this church one bit.

So far we have had chaos. Last night was one of the worst explosions. We came close to outright anger in our discussion.

But so far we have also been very much together. There is something there that keeps us together. I am convinced that it is God who drives us ahead in anger.

123

Last night the first demonstration of a changing, powerful God working in our midst, recreating out of chaos:

We had gathered about twenty couples together for supper. These were the people who we hoped would commit themselves before the meeting was over to leading a small group of people in their home in the discussion of church renewal. We had prepared a tape—a kind of characterization of the ineffectiveness of the church. We hoped this would stimulate discussion and be used by each of them in their own home discussion.

After playing the tape there was criticism:

"After hearing the tape it occurs to me that people in our discussion groups will say, 'Well, the church to me *means* all that activity: suppers, bazaars, picnics. . . . We enjoy doing it.' They will feel this is sufficient."

"It was too long [the tape]. I don't think you need this kind of stimulation. I didn't appreciate it. It made me think of a textbook that takes fifteen pages to get to the point. You could make the point much quicker through discussion."

"Are we going to use the tape in the discussion groups? I'm shocked. I don't think we ought to use it for discussion groups."

"I don't think this is the kind of tape to take into the small groups that we are talking about. We have interested people here. Once again we are talking to ourselves. The people who we need to reach are the ones who just drop their kids off at Church School. They are the ones who need to hear about renewal!"

At this point the objections mounted and we, who had spent so much time preparing for this evening, glanced at each other with defeat in our eyes. We needed these people to lead. If they didn't see the urgency of renewal we were finished—even before we started.

But then a strange thing happened. It was as if I were compelled to speak. I only once before felt that way and that was ten years ago at a Graham Crusade in New York. I know what it means in Acts, "and there appeared to them tongues as of fire"—I was on fire.

I am not too sure of all I said. I am sure I was filled with all kinds of emotions at that point. I was shocked at the response. I was disillusioned that people failed to see *themselves* in all this. I was just plain angry.

I said that when I had come from seminary I was filled with the idealistic notion that we had to organize the church to go forth into the world with banners flying. I said that I had imagined how as Christ's men and women we would participate in all the great causes through social action. I said that I wasn't here too long when I discovered how futile all this was because I had misunderstood the needs of the people who are already active in the church. I said something about the bleeding people that I had met here who needed to know about the healing power of Christ before they could go forth to heal. I said how much I had ached for those people and how I was tired of aching for them all alone. I said I had discovered how very much we needed one another for strength and sustenance and love and healing. I said that our aim was not to "involve" people but our aim was to learn and discover from one another how we might grow and help each other to be what we are meant to be. I guess I said a lot.

I believe God acted that night in a way that I have personally never witnessed before. People began to change right there.

"Our goals then are to examine ourselves and to try to discover what the church should be."

"I think I understand; I've learned that communicating love is what is important and that this is done best by allowing people a freedom to say what they think—this freedom I found in our Bible study group. If we can do this throughout the church we will really have something."

"I feel something here tonight. Something very sure and right and necessary, and I want to be a part of it. I have never felt this way before. I never knew what it meant to encounter God but now I think I'm beginning to understand."

"I'm with you in this. I think we need to reach people in a personal way and maybe this is just the way to do it."

A short while later, after some further discussion, we passed out commitment sheets and nineteen out of twenty couples signed the commitment to lead groups in discussion, while just a short half hour before it was unlikely that any would have signed.

God was there. God again created out of turmoil. From death He had given us life!

"I TELL YOU *that you must be born over again. The wind blows where it wills; you hear the sound of it, but you do not know where it comes from, or where it is going. So it is with everyone who is born from the spirit.*" JOHN 3:6,8 N.E.B.

SEVENTEEN GROUPS OF ten to twelve people in each group have gathered over a period of three to four weeks in the homes of the parish. How much genuine renewal there has been is hard to say.

Generally speaking, there has been little overall change. After the meetings ended, we slipped back into the same old grooves. Perhaps this is because we failed to encourage the groups to continue. We, in fact, deliberately broke them up and tried to re-form them around interest areas such as Bible study, teaching, youth, church property, community action. It was these groups that failed with one or two exceptions.

Looking back, I am sure that we missed the point. That is, nothing is going to happen without the presence of God here in our midst and in order for that to be so, we have to talk about Him somewhere down in the gut level. We have to express our feelings and anxieties about Him or it is no good at all. But we carefully designed Him right out of the meetings. In our desire to avoid offending the sensitivities of people who are too sophisticated to accept the real nature of God as the One who wants to change and rearrange and redirect the basic center of a man's life, we neatly avoided the subject. Instead of calling *ourselves* into question, we attempted to examine the church. This is safer. It is less likely to hurt or threaten as much if we center our complaints in an organization rather than on ourselves.

This is why the task is so unbelievably difficult. What is required is a reorientation of the human spirit, and we all want very much to resist a change so basic as that. We have already sacrificed too much and worked too hard and had our sights fixed too long on achieving success and prestige in the world. We simply will not hear of anything that will require us to remotivate our living. The arguments against change are far too logical and sensible for anyone to be deluded into taking the imperative of the Gospel too literally. Who wants to be meek and lowly and poor in spirit when the world so very much rewards vanity and superiority and dignity? The world proves the superiority of power and success—it's insane to even suggest the cross as an alternative.

Early in my life as an engineer I learned an axiom: Get the job done no matter what. Even if you sacrificed every human principle in the process it didn't matter, provided you accomplished the task. You painted a beautiful picture of success to the customer in spite of failure and incompetency in other respects. You demanded impossible things of the men who worked for you regardless of human feelings. You lied to and cheated the competition whenever you could. You played the game by any rules that were convenient if it meant getting the job done. It was a no-holds-barred world and if you didn't play it that way you were dead, you were on the bottom of the heap. Leo Durocher's quip, "Nice guys don't win ball games," was the philosophy of how to act in the business world.

And I very much played the game that way. For a while I led two lives. At meetings and committees in church I was the smiling, kindly, considerate soul who properly suppressed his anger and hostility and checked himself carefully for four-letter words before opening his mouth. At work I was quite the opposite. I was that hard-nosed, impersonal, get-the-job-done character that won the battles of business. I simply couldn't find the way of applying my new Christianity in either situation. At church I couldn't be myself for fear I wouldn't be accepted as a Christian, and at work I couldn't change the pattern that business had taught me for fear that any other approach would fail to accomplish the task. In both situations I was living a life that I thought the world I was in at the moment expected me to live. I was living the way I thought would be the most rewarding. There was really no difference in either case. I had learned the game well. I lived according to the rules of the moment. The rules that would award me the most points in my favor. So you see, deep down inside we don't want the Gospel. We don't want it for the very practical reason that we have been conditioned to think in terms of success measured by how much you are liked and how much wealth you have accumulated.

Let's face it, where is it going to get you if you go around forgiving everyone who fails to perform adequately ("Lord, how often shall my brother sin against me, and I forgive him?"—"I do not say to you seven times, but seventy times seven." Matthew 18:21-22)? What are the percentages in being benevolent to someone who is going to take you for all you've got ("If any one would sue you and take your coat, let him have your cloak as well." Matthew 5:40)? How perfectly impractical it is not to commit almost all our energies to obtaining the things we need ("Therefore I tell you, do not be anxious about your life, what you shall eat or what you shall drink, nor about your body, what you shall put on." Matthew 6:25). How far are you going to get in this world if you are too open and truthful about your feelings ("The truth will make you free." John 8:32)? What will sacrifice get you except heartache ("Take up [your] cross and follow me." Mark 8:34)?

You see, who in his right mind is going to subscribe to all

of that? No one! We can't possibly convince anyone that *this* is the way of life. It is too radical. It is too much opposed to *our* way of life. It is too unsure. No man will buy that.

So God must convince us. Somehow, in some mysterious way, God must come and sting us awake. He must open our eyes to the possibility that by some very incredible reason these are the real principles of success and joy and fulfillment. Because it's not obvious to any of us. These words of Jesus are just too incredible for anyone to believe or take seriously without a rude shaking of the foundations by God Himself.

Well, so we missed the point. That in itself is nothing new. People have been missing the point for centuries. But this is not to say we haven't made a beginning. This is not to say we didn't accomplish something in all this. Surely God was there in some of the corners at least. A few people who had long ago decided the church could care less about them are now showing some interest. Some people who were just plain lonely found new companionship and support. A few have gathered together around a common purpose: one group has begun to visit other people in the parish. A person or two has discovered a new relationship to God and the church that is fresh and meaningful. A number of people have begun to study the Bible for the first time in their lives. Much that is good and promising is occurring.

Perhaps the thing we have learned the most is that you cannot contrive an experiment in the laboratory, so to speak, which will demonstrate love, faith, hope, charity. You cannot contrive it because by definition these things are never contrived. We can create a situation in which the Spirit of God can move more freely and openly, but we cannot lead the

Spirit. We must play it loose enough so that the Spirit leads us. Maybe we didn't play it loose enough. Maybe it was too contrived. Maybe we tried too hard to mold people into shapes that *we* had decided were meaningful. Maybe we didn't quite trust God enough.

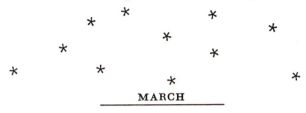

MARCH

Breakthrough!
It was at a youth folk night of all places. . . .
We invited kids from another church to join us for an evening of poetry, folk music with original tunes and words, readings, coffee, etc. But the guests took over the party. They bubbled over with the Spirit of Christ.

These kids were different than any I had met before who talked about prayer meetings and encounters with Jesus Christ. These were not Bible-toting, cliché-ridden, clean-cut, shirt-and-tie kids. These kids came through real. They excitedly talked about prayer sessions; how they got together in a big room, read something from the Bible, discussed it a bit, talked about who to pray for, got comfortable, turned out the lights (!) and prayed, sometimes for an hour.

Our coffee house was overwhelmed that night with this new and not completely understood enthusiasm. The joy was contagious and we resolved to take a trip to their church and find out just what this was all about.

In the car on the way home after joining their prayer meeting I heard comments like:

131

"I never knew God could seem so close."

"I really felt close to Him tonight and I felt I belonged to all those kids and most of them I didn't even know!"

"We just have to do this at our church. It was so beautiful and for the first time in my life I felt touched by God. I have always heard about God doing that but up until tonight I never believed a word of it."

"I just want to tell anyone who will listen about it."

APRIL

Breakthrough!

This from a member of one of our study groups:

"A long time ago I had a dream. In it I was touched by God. He had chosen me for a specific purpose. I always thought about that dream but it never seemed to happen. Sure, I went through the rituals: church on Sunday, teaching Sunday School, joining committees. But God didn't touch me. I didn't need Him. Life was enough without Him.

"Then I joined a study group. And every week I heard about 'experiences' and prayer and commitment. I think commitment bothered me the most. It kept hammering at me. I'd go home after a meeting and ask myself, 'Am I committed? What does it mean? How do I become committed?'

"Little by little I became aware of things. I saw Christ in people! This was exciting. But why couldn't *I* feel Christ? What was wrong with me? Where was Christ for *me?*

"I was praying differently. It wasn't just a habit with a mouthing or words. It was real; it was honest; I was asking Him for direction, for help in my search for Him.

"Then the change started. It was impossible for me to ignore a plea for help. I couldn't turn my back on poverty, prejudice, cruelty to human beings. I was growing!

"Finally, the time came for decision. Do I become totally involved in everything around me as Christ wants me to do, or should I stay safe and snug in my own little world and wait for a better time to begin?

"When I made my decision, the miracle happened. I felt Christ, I knew Christ, and for the first time in many months I knew joy!

"I think I know commitment now, and I thank God that I have finally been touched by Him."

MAY

Breakthrough!
Pentecost:
About fifteen kids worked up a service of worship to take to the hospital. They wanted communion so I went along. It was in the afternoon and I was exhausted from a tre-

mendous Pentecost celebration in our morning worship. I was not expecting very much and I wanted to get it over. I was sure it would be a typical disorganized, prayer-reading, monotone, deadly experience. I was never so surprised in my life.

How do you describe it? An expectant awareness and hopefulness seemed to come over me. We stood around the bed. These kids prayed individually. They confessed their weaknesses and how they had failed to be human and real and honest. They sang together; they shared their thoughts and music and words. When it came time for communion I did it very simply using very few words—it's amazing how much you can communicate with very few words. There was an expectant quiet there and I felt there was a presence that was very much beyond us. The thought rushed into my head that this must have been what it was like in the very early church: very simply, Christians gathered together. They prayed and spoke and sang; the sincerity, the spontaneity, the simple, quiet joy, the humanity of each one who stood there emerged in a sure small way. This was breakthrough indeed!

Breakthrough! What a joy to see it! How difficult it is to describe this encounter with God. Is it a sense of the Presence? If it is that alone, then perhaps it is the human mind playing its game. Is it a calling to a larger task in life, a compelling to become involved? If it is that alone, then perhaps it is a natural human feeling for a brother, a concern born out of observed need. Is it a desire to become more than we are? If it is that alone, then it would be ego perhaps. Is it the stimulation of poetry and verse, like great art or great music that digs deep down and touches some grand source of inspiration within the human soul? If it is that alone, then perhaps it is no more than Muzak or the dancing colors of psychedelic strobe.

Breakthrough is like all of these. And maybe that is why it is so rare, that is why it so often seems beyond reach, that is why that land of promise is so rarely visible—because God seems to be all mixed up with our humanity. He tangles Himself and involves Himself with our humanness. He rides in on our feelings, our mind's eye, our desire to lead significant lives, our human spirit, our tears over a brother burned. And we fail to see Him, because we insist more often than not that the breakthrough is our doing rather than His. We miss the incarnation. We do not yet realize just how far God is prepared to go to avoid overpowering us, protecting our individuality with His loving Spirit.

But couldn't it just be a little more often? Couldn't God have biased things a little more toward the positive, toward the joy, making the good more obvious and inviting? In His wisdom, I suppose, it is best as it is. After all, am I the creator? Like Job I was not there when the earth's foundations were laid. So I suppose it is best as it is.

It's just that it would be nice if breakthrough were not so rare or difficult to come by or to understand or to believe.

AND THE LORD *said to him [Moses], "This is the land of which I swore to Abraham, to Isaac, and to Jacob, "I will give it to your descendants." I have let you see it with your eyes, but you shall not go over there."* DEUTERONOMY 34:4 R.S.V.

O Lord, can I be an instrument of your grace?
Is that too much to ask?
I know you have given me the ability to see things
as they should be,

135

But is that grace?
Perhaps.
Perhaps it is because without seeing me like I ought
to be I would become unbearably righteous.
Perhaps it is because to see the possibilities is the
only way there is movement and change and hope.
Perhaps it is because someone needs to catch the
vision to keep it alive.

But why is breakthrough so rare?
Why does it so often seem that the promise is just
beyond fingertips?
Why is it given to some to see, but not to go over
there?
'Tis enough!
'Tis enough to see, isn't it, Lord?
I am satisfied to see and reach and see and reach and
see . . . and reach . . . and see . . . and reach.

At least I say I am . . . satisfied.
But honestly, there is something
Within
That is never
Satisfied.
I wonder,
Is . . .
That . . .
You,
Lord?

EPILOGUE

EPILOGUE

OBVIOUSLY, THE STORY is not
finished. It will never really be finished,
anymore than any church or Christian is completed on this
earth. And so, rather than a success story, I would like to
think of it as a struggle toward success, in the best sense of
that word. It is a struggle for insight, inspiration, understanding, and honesty. A wrestling, so to speak, sort of like
Jacob's wrestling with the angel. It is God's striving with us
and our (my) resistance to His enlistment of us under the
sign of the cross, with the real question being whether we
will prevail in our struggle with God and with men as
Jacob did.

My observation is that most churches and preachers do
not prevail. Wherever you look there is an inevitable compromise, a readjustment to reality, a kind of quiet giving
in to the immense and seemingly unmovable resistance to
the Gospel.

And this is quite understandable. I read the Gospel and I
see its impossible message which is in stark contrast to what
we are and what we *really* believe in and I am awe-struck
by the difference. I look at our comfortable condition and
wonder how we will ever be willing to risk what we have,
especially when most are too materially secure and too emo-

tionally insecure to even relinquish the most minor concessions to one another. I look at the needs of people and conclude that they far outweigh their ability to serve in any real way other than the most superficial committee or church program. And so I understand why we compromise and dilute the New Testament and make it easy and weak and wide. What other alternative is there?

I suppose someone will point out that there is a certain pessimism contained in these pages and they will be right. And if anyone should say Christianity is not supposed to be pessimistic, they may be right again. But if the pessimism comes through it is because I've tried to be honest about the parish and myself. I have discovered that when we begin to be honest, then God has a chance of breaking in and changing things. It is only when we really see ourselves as we are that any change is going to occur. And, in fact, I believe that our very honesty, the revelation of what we are, is always God himself present in our lives.

But I am convinced that it is not an easy matter for anyone to face up to reality, especially for us who have too much material wealth and too little confidence in anything "spiritual" to really accept Christ's way completely. We are simply not going to do this in suburbia because we have too much to lose and we are too threatened by the change. We simply don't want to change. So, the real facts are: no amount of talking, no amount of clever reasoning, no amount of logical preaching, no amount of efficient programs, no amount of clever denominationalism is going to make any real difference. It may stimulate a few to come to church a little more often and it may keep the church busy—but it is

140

not really going to change anything because deep down inside *we don't want the God revealed in the Bible!*

As far as I can conclude, the liberal point of view is not the way to achieve any real change in the parish. (And I say this with many reservations because I believe in much of liberalism—its freedom and acceptance, for instance.) But it fails because it places too much emphasis on man's ability to recognize his own condition and correct it (as if he even wanted to!). It assumes too much maturity. For all his humanism the liberal has a certain naiveté about people and what really motivates them.

But if liberalism fails, fundamentalism fails even more miserably to change anything. It fails because it narrows ideas and beliefs. It limits so much the place of man to think and reason and act that he has little chance to grow and mature and discover real freedom *from*, so that he can be free *for*.

What we need is the openness of the liberal and the conversion of the fundamentalist. We need to freely open up the doors and windows of life and let a cool, fresh breeze into all the musty corners in order that the wind of the Spirit may come in too. We need conversion without hanging on it all the stifling trappings of orthodoxy and denominationalism and traditions. Christ has to break in somehow to enable us to rise above (not abandon) reason and logic and so enable us to commit ourselves to the foolishness of The Way.

Harvey Cox writes in the last chapter of his excellent book, *The Secular City,* about how Bonhoeffer suggests that *we* have to make the decision. He says, "He [Bonhoeffer] makes us answer for ourselves whether the God of the Bible is real or is just a rich and imaginative way man has fashioned to talk about himself. No amount of verbal clarification can set this disagreement aside. In the last analysis it is not a matter of clear thinking at all but a matter of personal decision. Luther was right: deciding on this question is a matter, which, like dying, every man must do for himself." But this, I believe, is precisely where we fail. We expect that we are going to make our own irrational choice, while all along the choice is impossible for us to make. And so long as we believe we are going to make it there is going to be very little movement, very little real change. Why? Because so long as we believe we will choose, our tactics will be to logically convince ourselves by some technique or logical argument. We will argue ourselves into it. But experience has shown that this simply does not work. It does not work because we are *not* that mature. We either cannot, or we do not want to stand on our own hind legs. Contrary to Bonhoeffer, we have not "come of age" in terms of maturity, and perhaps the logical outcome of Bonhoeffer's famous final words is the idea of the death of God simply because the mistaken evaluation of our maturity has led to a blind alley. No one changes by his own volition; it is God who changes us in the last analysis after all.

How then does this change come? Answering that question is what the struggle is all about. Jacob asked the angel his name; that is to say, he wanted some answers. And the angel refused. So it is with us. There are no *easy* answers. They simply will not drop out of heaven—nor out of our church boards and agencies, nor through this program or that. The Spirit blows where it wills. Yet I am utterly convinced that this change is most likely to come when people begin to seriously attempt to understand one another; that is, when even in the most limited and superficial way the inhibitions and fears begin to fade ever so slightly, then God is most likely going to be able to do something with us.

And there is no reason we should fear the struggle because this is precisely how we come to know God the best. We must remember that Jacob wrestled all night before he received God's blessing. It was *after* the wrestling match that the angel blessed Jacob. I have been pessimistic; I have been disillusioned; I have been ready to give it all up; I have said to myself that I must have been out of my mind to have given up so much for so little. But, curiously, in the struggle God has become *real* for me. I know who my Lord is. Like Job, I would say, "I had heard of thee by the hearing of the ear, but now my eye sees thee." Over these years I have become utterly convinced of the presence of God in Christ Jesus. So maybe the conversion we need comes best through struggle and turmoil. If that is so, the task is there before us and it is not easy.

We live in critical times. As I write this the greatest crisis in this country is racial, and what is needed is a change in attitude—but that is not going to happen without bitter struggle and upheaval. It never does, not really, not permanently. Perhaps Martin Luther King is our best modern example of that. And Christ Himself is that towering statement by God that somehow and for some reason there is in the midst of life a cross upon which God dwells and from which God comes in the most profound and real and loving and magnificent way imaginable.

*

*   *